FLY FISHING TECHNIQUES

FLY FISHING TECHNIQUES

Basic Fundamentals and Championship Form

ALF WALKER

Pagurian Press Limited
TORONTO

ISBN 0-88932-002-0
Printed and bound in United States of America

Dedication

This book is dedicated to the many friends I have fished with and to those who, during pleasant hours, have shared with me their thoughts, experiences, and theories on fly fishing.

It is especially for those who, I trust, will find the volume useful in their search for a simple introduction to the casting of a fly, and establish a speedy initiation into the totally absorbing pleasure the sport provides. Hopefully, it will create a solid basic platform on which to base their own investigation and experimentation.

It is for those who contributed so much to my angling education during my formative years — not that I have ever ceased to learn — a humble tribute to fishermen with whom, sadly, I shall "nae see, nor cast a flee, nor fish alang wae agin" . . . at least not from this bank of the river.

And finally it is for my wife who has viewed my complete involvement in angling with limitless patience and the kindest of understanding and to the memory of my father who introduced me to the pastime.

Acknowledgments

This work has been undertaken in an attempt to introduce the subject of fly fishing in a manner that will speedily acquaint newcomers to the angling form. It has been written in a style that is hoped will be easily understood and be of service to all who seek to sample the enthralling pastime of fly fishing the world over. It was compiled to supply a background of information that will perhaps prove of interest to the followers of the sport, covering the basic principles of the angling method and the rudimentary techniques, together with a scattering of knowledge surrounding the evolution of fly fishing which may provide a basis for thought, development, and individual experiment.

The contents are compiled from personal experience, and the contact I have been fortunate to have with innumerable angling friends. I should like to acknowledge, in particular, (starting from my earliest years) the members of the Seaton Burn, Hartford, and Bedlington and Blagdon Angling Clubs; The Northumbrian Anglers' Federation; the principals of J. B. Walker; John Robertson; W. & H. Temple and "The Fishing Hut"; The British Casting Association, The Scottish Casting Association, The Scottish Recreational Council, and the British Tackle Dealers Association, The Toronto Anglers and Hunters Association, The Outdoor Writers of Canada, and the Izaak Walton Club of Oakville, Ontario.

It is appropriate that I extend special thanks to Len. Borgström, President of ABU Svangsta, Sweden; James W. MacCallum, Managing Director of ABU Great Britain; G. Allan Burton, Chief Executive of The Robert Simpson Company of Canada; the members of the Restigouche Fishing Club; James L. Hardy, of The House of Hardy, (and the rest of my good friends) in Alnwick, England; Harold Sharpe of Farlow Sharpe, Aberdeen, Scotland; Wolff Wahle, A. E. Partridge, Redditch, England; Ted. Wyatt, "Eagle Claw," Wright & McGill, Barrie, Ontario; O. Mustad & Son, Gjøvik, Norway, and Geo. Day of Essential Agencies who is the Canadian agent for Mustad; Bob Logan of "Beacham's," Toronto, the representative of Hardy and Farlow Sharpe in Canada; Bill Hudson of Graycombe Associates,

Mississauga, Ontario; Rod Towsley of Berkley and Co.; Stanley E. Bogdan, Custom Reels, Nashua, U.S.A.; Arthur L. Walker, Reel Maker, Farmingdale, New York; Scientific Anglers, Midland, Mich., U.S.A.; Tycoon Fin-Nor, Miami, Florida; Jerome J. Knap; "Red" Cohen; Charles Wade; Bill Tredway of the Greenbank Trout Club; Elliott G. Deighton who assisted with the instructional photography, and finally to Glenn Edward Witmer, Managing Director of the publishing company who gave me the opportunity to write the book.

In the reading there may be found avenues of thought and aspects of the sport where some possibly will not agree with me, but this fact itself is, I feel, what must surely be rated as one of the finest facets of fishing — a philosophy I borrow unblushingly from Jim Green of the Fenwick Rod Company — and leave with my readers for consideration.

Contents

All line drawings appearing in this book are by the author.

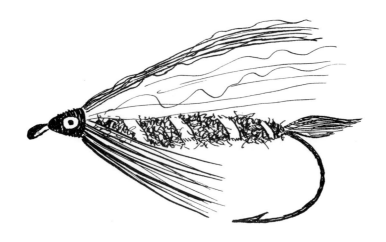

Introduction

The technique of fly fishing as we know it today almost certainly evolved from the fishing for trout in the distant past.

In the writings of Aelian in the third century, there are contained what must be the first written details of a fly pattern, and the materials with which to dress it; the instructions as to how it should be fished; and where, on a certain Macedonian river, he had seen the angling method applied. The writer speaks of "spotted fish, the food of which consists of insects that fly about the river, that can be caught by wrapping red wool about a hook and tying to it a pair of waxy cock feathers to imitate the wings. Using a reed six-feet long, and a line of the same length, to which the fly is attached, the line is dropped upon the surface of the water, where the fish seize the fly and are thus captured."

It would be quite a reasonable assumption to make that this angling form developed from attempts to catch certain types of fish, which were observed by the ancient fishermen to be feeding on a surface food supply of floating insects, and it would naturally lead to experimentation and eventual success by those early anglers. Aelian had obviously witnessed the method of fishing and, thankfully, found it of sufficient interest to chronicle the event, an act for which he has been given first place in the annals of fly-fishing literature by later exponents of the art. There is nothing more written on the subject until the fifteenth century.

I find the twelve centuries of silence intriguing and, having spent many moments of reverie pondering the matter, and rather than admit to the loss of the art in its infancy, I fondly cling to a personal theory based along these lines:

In the third century, when Aelian recorded the first descriptions of fly fishing, the Roman Empire was still near its zenith. Is it not possible that, mixed in with the hordes of traders and soldiers who constituted the spread of civilization, there were a few individuals who knew of the art of catching spotted fish that took food in the form of insects from the surface of the water?

In western Europe, for example, was there an occasion when a bronze pin from a toga, sheep's wool, hen feathers, horse hair, and a slender willow branch cut from the bank of the stream provided the equipment? A side-arm throw made to place the feathered lure on to the water, and a spotted, surface-feeding fish landed by the use of the Macedonian technique? It is safe to speculate that even as the primary object of the exercise was to provide sustenance, there was a certain amount of skill, satisfaction, enjoyment, and pride taken in performing the task, a form of primitive elation, while catching fish for food.

If such a theory is acceptable, then it will not be too difficult to imagine such a scene enacted on some remote Northumbrian stream, close to the Great Wall of Hadrian, by some Roman centurion on an overseas tour of duty. The act of angling was closely observed by a Pict servant boy in attendance, while the Roman officer bemoaned the fact that in the southern part of the country the fish in the clear chalk streams were larger and fed more readily, that his Celtic attendant had been a much better ghillie, and that his previous post in Macedonia had a more pleasant climate.

Once seen, the skill could easily be learned and passed on. And so, I fondly like to think, the style of angling was perpetuated, although, with the departure of the Roman legions and the chaos that followed, possibly it became a jealously-guarded skill, hidden within the monastic system.

In ancient Egypt during the golden era of the Pharoahs, by Royal Decree, sport fishing with rod and line was an activity in which only those of high lineage could partake. Such was their regard for the pastime . . . a relaxation only for the gods. Meanwhile, the rest of the population in the kingdom bordering the Nile had to be content to use hand lines, nets, or spears. This fact leads me to my previous conclusion: the skill of fly fishing was absorbed into what was to be the roots of civilization after the departure of the Romans from Britain. The Romans left behind them, in a dark void of upheaval and lawlessness, tiny sparks of enlightenment, the cultural and religious centers which later developed into monasteries, where, with other aspects of knowledge, the skill of catching a fish with a fly was preserved during the silent centuries. All conjecture, admittedly. However, the romanticism is allowable if a twelve-hundred-year period, devoid of all information, is not to be ignored, and the loss of the art recorded in the third century, accepted.

The next text to use an angling form that used artificial flies to catch fish is the *Second Book of St. Albans,* printed in 1496, which contains "The Treatise of Fishing with an Angle" that lists twelve flies. It is attributed to Dame Juliana Berners, Prioress of the Nunnery of Sopwell, near the Abbey Town of St. Albans.

Not until 1676, in the fifth edition of *The Compleat Angler* by Izaak Walton, does the technique of fly fishing in written form show advancement. The section contributed by Charles Cotton (who describes himself as "the adopted son and friend" of Walton), "Instruction to Angle for a Trout or Grayling in a Clear Stream", lists over sixty patterns of flies and his lucid description of tying a fly is a delight to read.

There is no doubt that Cotton was an avid fly fisherman and the text written by him is the next significant record concerning the development of the art of fly fishing from that given in the *Book of St. Albans.* Indeed, Cotton with his infectious, enthusing, and quite undeliberate and innocent manner, and with the obvious affinity he had for the technique, elevated the angling form above the normal bait-fishing methods.

In the realms of fly fishing the name of Charles Cotton must stand to the fore. But it is the name of Walton that lives on, while that of Cotton occupies a much lesser niche in the general regard. However, analyzing the deep friendship that existed between these two anglers and a further consideration of the situation, the title of the Father of Angling resting on Walton is one that Cotton most surely would have wished.

From 1800 onwards, development of equipment, advancement of technique, and documentation of the angling form increased, providing a tremendous reservoir of information for those interested in fly fishing. Today we have a truly massive library to draw from, where a wealth of knowledge lies stored within the covers of innumerable books, and embraces every facet connected with the angling form.

The enormous contributions of Halford and Hewitt; the lyrical words of Sir Edward Grey; the concise detail of Gordon, Skues and LaBranche; the masterly and monumental output of McClane; the incomparable style of Gringrich; the scholarly work of Bergman and Brooks; the heritage of Moseley, Ronalds, Kite, Jennings, Marinaro, and Flick; the superb product of Schwiebert; the flair of Wulff; the innovative methods of Wright, Swisher, and Richards . . . not only does the fly fisherman have an engrossing sport to pursue, he has an equally absorbing area of interest provided in the literature connected with it.

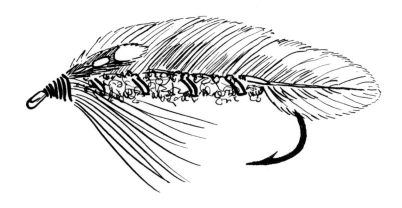

CHAPTER 1

The Relationship between Equipment and Technique

It is the rhythmic and interesting casting style, and the rather mysterious and intriguing angling form that attract so many fishermen to fly fishing, which, once tried and savored, is a taste rarely forsaken. Fly casting opens entirely new and exciting dimensions of angling.

While other forms of angling, such as surf fishing or bait-casting with a multiplier, spinning with a fixed-spool reel in fresh or salt water, spin-casting with a closed-face reel of the push-button type, or bait fishing with a simple center-pin reel, all require a compact weight at the end of the line to enable a cast to be executed, with fly fishing it is the *line that is cast.*

The fly line is really an extremely pliable, elongated "weight" and, whereas in other types of angling it is the compact weight on the end of the line which loads the rod on the compression stroke of the cast, it is the fly line which provides the resistance necessary to flex the limber rods used by fly fishermen. A compact weight is thrown out to the front of an angler from the rear with a casting action consisting of one motion. A fly line is cast back and forth, while the fisherman feeds line or retrieves it until he has the desired extended length before placing the line on to the water. A flexible rod is used to push and pull the line through the air, to which is attached a leader and, on the end of it, a fly (neither of which have significant weight).

Successful fly casting, and fly fishing depend to a great extent on the efficiency of the equipment (at this point ignoring the adroitness of the angler's skill, and dealing solely with the tackle).

The function of a fishing rod is, in a rudimentary form, both that of a *lever* and a *spring;* basically a fishing rod can be described as both a casting tool and an angling implement.

A rod made to cast a compact weight is generally shorter and stiffer. Angling performance leans towards the lever principle, while a rod produced to cast a fly line is longer and much more flexible. Therefore it is more like a spring. These two elements, lever and spring, are the factors which, when combined, control the action a rod produces. For the casting of a fly,

14

greater rod resilience is a definite requirement, as opposed to the throwing of a weight, where a more positive firmness is desirable.

"Balanced" fly-fishing equipment is essential if the highest potential is to be realized, and the maximum of efficiency utilized on any level of expertise. *Balance,* when applied to modern fly-fishing equipment is simply matching the *correct weight of line* to a suitable and corresponding *power of rod.* If balance does relate to a point where an assembled rod, reel, and line, when laid upon an outstretched finger, finds the weight has an equalized distribution at a spot within an inch or so from the top of the handle, it is secondary to the matching of the correct *line weight to rod power.*

There is small chance of a mis-marriage of a fly rod and fly line, by the present standards used by the line-making and rod-producing companies (established by the American Fishing Tackle Manufacturer's Association). All lines are classified within a numerical system based on weight plus an initial code which specifies line type and profile (double taper, shooting taper, level, or weight forward) and function (floating or sinking). A power assessment number is put on fly rods; thus the task of selection has been greatly simplified.

Before this system was internationally accepted, lines were listed according to size, designated by numbers. They were superseded by a diameter code that could also denote line profile. The diameter code eventually created chaos when new line-making materials were introduced. For example, when lines of identical thickness made of nylon, silk, and dacron were marked with the same code, it was found that a line in silk would suit a particular rod, while a nylon line was too light for it, and the dacron line too heavy, yet they were all carrying the same alphabetical code. The establishment of the A.F.T.M.A. formula solved all balance problems.

In the years following the creation of the line and rod selection system, a generalized, yet very sound selection situation has evolved relating rod power and length to line weight. There are, of course, certain specialized techniques where rod specification and line classification do not conform. However, most requirements are contained in the following Chart which gives in detail the generalized relationship: the range of A.F.T.M.A. line classification, codes, and numerical rod power and length, and also illustrates line profiles.

Line Type and Designation Initial Code			
F	floating	**D.T.**	double taper
S	sinking	**W.F.**	weight forward
S/F	sinking floating	**S.T.**	shooting taper
I	intermediate	**L**	level

A Guide to Line Weight and Rod Length

A.F.T.M.A. Fly Line Code	Line Weight: first 30 ft. in grains	Generalized Rod Length	Power Classification
3	100	5'6"-6'6"	3
4	120	6'-7'	4
5	140	7'-7'6"	5
6	160	7'6"-8'6"	6
7	185	7'6"-8'6"	7
8	210	8'-9'	8
9	240	8'6"-9'6"	9
10	280	9'-10'	10
11	330	9'-9'6"	11
12	380	9'-9'6"	12

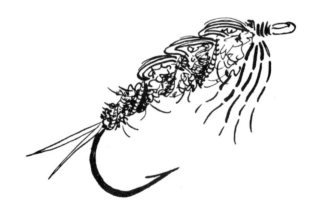

CHAPTER 2

The Tackle

The basic equipment of the fly fisherman the world over, whether he fishes for trout or tarpon, is rod, reel, line, fly, and leader. To be more specific, it is necessary to have: a rod of suitable length and of sufficient power to perform each type of angling application efficiently; a line (be it floating or sinking, double tapered or weight forward) of a similar numerical weight assessment to the strength of the rod, the choice being made according to that which the fishing situation demands; a light, reliable reel of sufficient line capacity; a tapered leader of adequate strength; and a well-tied fly on the correct size of hook with which to catch the fish.

Equipment has progressed from the primitive tools of the earliest times, when a fly was thrown on to the water attached to a six-foot length of line tied to a six-foot long reed, to today's highly developed, extremely efficient, and sophisticated tackle which embraces all avenues of fly casting.

Fishing with feathered insect imitations (dry flies), and aquatic life forms (wet flies, nymphs, and streamers) for trout and salmon continues to progress and attracts a greater following every season. However, the gradual discovery — now developing into an avalanche — *that any predatory fish can be caught with a feathered lure* of one kind or another (still to all intents and purposes a fly); and the realization that fly-fishing equipment offers the most angling interest, the greatest fishing challenge, and the most satisfactory piscatorial rewards, has opened up a new realm of angling.

The creation of a new fly design, the discovery of a new angling style, the development of a new method, the establishment of a new technique that will catch a new species of fish with a fly rod or will increase the ability of anglers to catch a type already known to take a fly, continues at an amazing rate. Each breakthrough is a barrier overcome, another step forward, as a new fly-fishing zone is opened to the brotherhood of the fly rod.

Be it casting a fly for mackerel in Scotland, pike in Canada, rainbow trout in New Zealand, bass in the United States, bonefish in Mexico, grayling in Alaska, brown trout in Chile, tarpon in Costa Rica — fly fishermen will be found enjoying their sport to the full.

THE ROD

The fly rod is an item of the fly fisherman's equipment that must be discussed in detail. For most anglers it is more than an essential item of fishing equipment, it is an article of fishing gear held in high regard. Just as a violinist has an almost spiritual relationship with his violin, so a fly fisherman eventually develops a similar affinity to his fly rods.

It might even be said that a fly rod has character and personality, rather than power and action. The hand-built split-cane rods from the past, bearing such illustrious and cherished names as Leonard, Hardy, Thomas, Walker-Bampton, and Payne, are treated with great reverence which, because of their extremely good angling performance, superb casting ability, and the high degree of craftsmanship they exemplify, represent a glorious era in angling history and are fast becoming collectors' pieces.

A fly rod normally consists of two sections of equal or occasionally uneven lengths (for convenience in transportation), which have a joint fitting of some kind that unites the sections when the rod is assembled. There are, of course, three-sectioned fly rods and the modern "pack rod" which may consist of up to five or six sections.

Ideally, I suppose, a rod should be in one piece. However, the advantages of a rod without joints do not justify the inconvenience of transporting and storing a fragile eight or nine-foot length.

Some rods are occasionally supplied with extra tip sections, although this practice dates back to the days when manufacturing processes, material treatments, and bonding agents were inferior to those of the present day, and the two tips, being the weakest sections of the rod, were intended to be used alternately. Today, a spare-tip section is unnecessary, save for replacement of a broken top section and, from my experience, it is invariably the spare top piece that is accidentally damaged or broken, usually when the slender section is left vulnerable and alone in a cloth rod bag after the rod has been assembled.

A metal or plastic protective case or tube is a good investment, although care must be taken not to damage line guides when inserting the rod into the container. Never drop a rod into a tube — always hold the tube at an angle and slide the rod in carefully.

Ferrules

The joints which connect the sections of a fly rod can be grouped within four basic methods of union: the metal suction ferrule, the internal spigot, the external sleeve, and the splice.

A craftsman of many years' experience making a metal suction ferrule for a split bamboo rod in Aberdeen, Scotland.

The metal ferrule consists of two tubes, one a tight push fit in the other. The smaller, the male joint, is attached to the base of the upper section of the rod; the larger, the female joint, is fitted to the uppermost portion of the lower section. When the two are united, they produce a perfectly good and time-proven method of rod assembly. Steel, brass, and silver-based metals are all used as materials for metal ferrules.

Over the years, wear will cause the male joint to work free. When this happens, a light tap with a blunt instrument to produce a slightly oval area will solve the problem.

In the past, metal ferrules had locking devices with screw-lock and spring stud-lock systems, neither of which have stood the test of time. There were also tenon extension pieces projecting from the lower part of the male ferrule that slotted into a recess situated at the bottom of the female aperture to create a more positive fitting. These have long been discarded as unnecessary embellishments in modern ferrule design.

An internal spigot is used to marry sections of a rod made from a tapered tubular shaft. A union is created by a tapered peg anchored in the top part of the lower section. The peg, being of a similar diameter as the inside measurements of the tube that forms the upper section, provides a tight push fit and is a most satisfactory rod junction for tubular rods. When it eventually wears, the spigot joint can be tightened by removing with a file, a tiny portion of the lower part of the upper rod section, thereby inserting the peg fractionally farther into the section above.

The External Sleeve

The external sleeve uses individually tapered tubular shafts which produce a wedge union to fit the rod section together. The shafts which provide this unique wedge fit have extremely critical tapers, the external diameters of the taper of the lower section matching identically the internal measurements of the upper sections.

This type of rod-section assembly is tremendously efficient. Any wear that does occur is simply absorbed by a more positive seating of the section above, on to that which is below.

The external sleeve is a natural method of joining tubular rod shafts. Solely as a matter of interest, it is worth mentioning an upside-down metal ferrule-type known as the Irish Ferrule, which dates back to the nineteenth century. It had the male joint on the top of the butt section and the female on the lower part of the upper section. This was a clever attempt to solve the problem of marrying two pieces of rod, the lower of which had a diameter similar to that above, without removing too much wood from either section or producing a ferrule that did not cause too large an obtrusion and spoil the visual appearance of the rod.

Ferrule Types

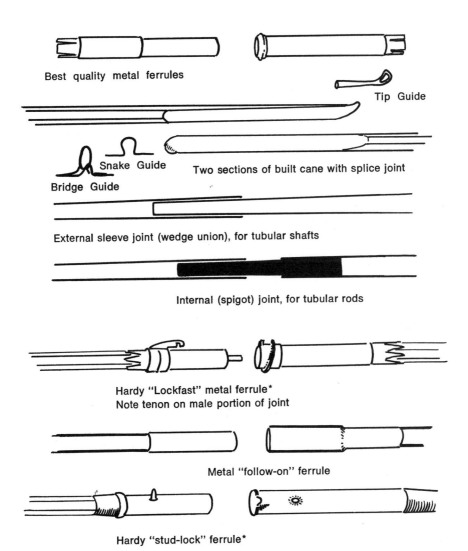

Best quality metal ferrules

Tip Guide

Snake Guide

Bridge Guide

Two sections of built cane with splice joint

External sleeve joint (wedge union), for tubular shafts

Internal (spigot) joint, for tubular rods

Hardy "Lockfast" metal ferrule*
Note tenon on male portion of joint

Metal "follow-on" ferrule

Hardy "stud-lock" ferrule*

*These two styles of joint are no longer in production. Rods with these types of ferrule are still in use, and stand testimony to the craftsmanship of another era.

It should also be noted that there are now modern "follow-on" metal joints which allow identical diameter sections (a cut tubular rod blank for example) to be fitted perfectly and speedily, without either material being removed or packing added to achieve the correct fit.

Only a solid material, such as built cane or greenheart — once a premier wood for the manufacture of fly rods — can be used for a splice joint. It is done by cutting a sloping face on the ends of the rod sections that are to be attached to each other. These angled four to six-inch faces are a perfect fit, one upon the other, and the two pieces are bound together with tape. This method of rod assembly still finds favor in Scotland and Scandinavia for long, three-section salmon fly rods, and possibly provides the only true "one piece action claim" from two and three-section rods, because the area of section union does actually flex. The spigot and sleeve advocates claim that these systems produce a near one piece action. However, any union with sufficient strength and rigidity to create a satisfactory sectional joint does not offer much more — other than less weight perhaps — than the efficiency of the metal ferrule. They are all excellent jointing methods. It is up to the angler to select whichever ferrule style he prefers.

ROD-MANUFACTURING PROCESSES

The action a fly rod produces in the hand while angling and casting is filled with intangibles; personal assessments tend to become involved: vague words such as "backbone" and "sweetness" are often connected with the performance of the rod, and terms such as "bite" and "steely" are used.

Mass produced, tubular fly rods with a tapered shaft construction outsell all others, although the traditional material, split bamboo, has always been regarded as better by a smaller, more discriminating number of anglers. Built cane is in the process of enjoying a resurgence of popularity. The medium-quality tubular rod is less than one-third the cost of a split bamboo rod. It has put the equipment necessary to cast a fly within the financial reach of everyone, a fact which possibly has been one of the major influencing factors in the explosion of interest in fly fishing and the growing number of anglers it is attracting.

Remember, a fly rod is initially a lever and a spring: a casting tool and a fishing implement. It should fish well and cast efficiently — throw a fly, land a fish, and provide the angler with a decisive yet sensitive link to the line, the fly — and hopefully, a fish!

Dry fly and wet fly-rod action are terms once related to the construction of split-bamboo rods made earlier in the century. A rod which produced a stiff, fast, lever-like casting action to throw off moisture from the line and dry off the fly was the first choice of the dry fly fisherman, while a rod with a slow, soft, spring-like action was the type chosen by the wet fly angler in order that fly and line, by retaining moisture, would sink on delivery to the stream.

The design of the modern fly rod, with its superior taper and material, has produced a middle-of-the-road action, midway between the old stiff dry fly rods, and the soft wet fly rods, which now combines the virtues of both. This feature of rod development and progress, when combined with the present-day advances in fly-line technology where a certain line is made to float and another to sink are features which lines previously could not emulate. They have immensely improved tackle for fly fishing. In the past, the rod had to assist the angling application, a stiff rod for dry fly and a soft action for wet fly. The chosen method of angling, be it surface presentation or sunk work, is now decided by the line and not the rod.

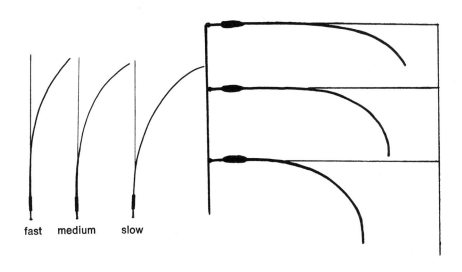

fast   medium   slow

Conventional Action Rods   **Fast Progressive Taper**

Of course there are still stiff, powerful, heavy-action rods made for long casts, large flies, and big fish, and long, willow-like, light, delicate rods produced for tiny flies, fine leaders, and extra control. The few rods of this type that are still manufactured today are an honest reflection of market demand, and as is true of any hyper-specialized area . . . are available at a price.

Always consider a rod to be a combination of spring and lever, a casting tool and a fishing implement, and the "action" — the way it throws a line, the manner in which it assists angling — the feel of the rod in the hand, as the "temperament": fast, critical, responsive, fastidious, or, slow, flattering, sensitive, and appreciative both to the art of casting and the application to angling.

23

Fly rod action can be defined to a certain degree. Actions described as conventional, through action, full action, parabolic, apply when rod movement utilizes the full length of the rod. The terms fast, medium, and slow are associated with them, while progressive action and compounded tapers are forms of true flexibility that move down the rod in varying degrees under the application of an assortment of stresses. Rods of this type normally have a tippy feel, and a very fast action.

To better explain the first group of rod actions, imagine three rods of similar power assessment, but described as fast, medium, and slow, all flexed under a similar compression load (either casting a line, or playing a fish); but with the second type, the flex of one rod, subjected to three different compression weights.

A longer rod is more useful to the tyro, say for example, a Class Six eight footer for trout, rather than a shorter version of Class Six in a six footer which is sometimes the choice of the expert. The chart showing the generalized rod length and power classification should be consulted if the need arises.

Awareness, the transmission of feel in a rod, is an area that receives great attention in fly-fishing circles and is a very personal matter. However, rods made from split bamboo have the ability to transmit a greater degree of "feel" from the fly to the hand, appreciably more than the vast majority of rods of a tubular construction produced from a tapered mandrel.

In the main, bamboo rods are solid in construction, although some of the more expensive are hollow. They consist of six tapered triangular sections of Tonkin cane, cut from the hard densely-fibered outer surface of the cane, and are placed together with the toughest facial section outwards, the softer area to the center, and with the nodes of the bamboo staggered throughout the length of the rod for maximum strength and uniformity of flex. The segments are glued together. With most cane rods today, a further process, impregnation, is carried out on the split-bamboo rod blanks. This treatment consists of boiling the built cane-rod sections in shellac, a process which makes the rod impervious to heat and damp, and greatly prolongs its life.

It would be wise, if buying a split bamboo rod that an impregnated type be considered, for it is much more durable than an untreated version which may, however, be perfectly suitable in temperate zones such as Western Europe. In climates where there is extreme, dry cold or humid heat a regular-built rod will not provide a normal life span in, for example, East Africa, Canada, or South America.

The story of the impregnation process is rather interesting, and the version I shall relate was told to me by Harold Sharpe, the rod builder of Aberdeen, Scotland, as we tested rods from his workshop on the River Dee, only a few miles from the benches of his craftsmen.

In his Aberdeen factory, Harold Sharpe is shown checking the taper of a built cane rod section.

This is the tale that Harold told me: During the early days of World War II, the frames of most fighter planes and light bombers were made of wood, for lightness and, naturally, for greater strength with less weight, the frames were of a laminated construction. Vibration, however, played havoc with all joints. To solve the problem of bolted angle joints actually disintegrating from vibrational stresses, they experimented by boiling the sections of air-frame corners in shellac, an impregration process that considerably strengthened the timber laminations, strengthened them to such a degree that, whereas the sectional joins in the air-frame were then standing up to the stress, the connecting sections were not and eventually all parts of the laminated frame, subject to stress, were treated in this manner. The idea was "borrowed" by the split-bamboo manufacturers, who immediately recognized the potential the process lent to built cane. When rod making started again after the end of hostilities, the impregnation feature was hailed as a tremendous advance in the technique of cane-rod building by fly fishermen the world over.

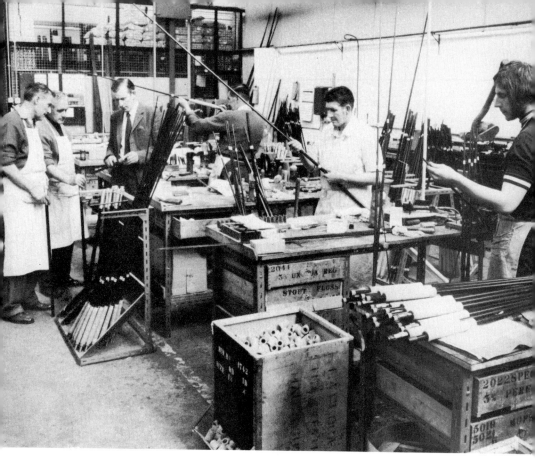

A scene in an assembly area for tubular rod shafts in the Hardy factory in Alnwick, Northumberland.

The tapers of split-bamboo rods control the distribution of weight, as cane is a natural material, whereas it is the wall thickness and taper of tubular rods made from glass fiber and thermo-plastic resins, (synthetic compounds), which decide rod power and action. Weight and taper are factors which today are computer controlled, and it is this most sophisticated technological development that has ultimately been responsible for a phenomenal improvement in fly-rod performance and quality, together with better adhesives and still finer machinery to produce the equipment.

The quality of craftsmanship, the high degree of skill, the years of experience, and the number of hours that it takes to make split-bamboo rods are reasons why a built-cane rod is so expensive. Complex, mass-production methods make available the tapered tubular shafts of the synthetic rod blanks, excellent pieces of angling equipment, at a more economical price. It is rather like choosing between leather or vinyl, silk or polyester, plastic or pottery. There are really very few poor quality rods

The creation of a tubular fiber-glass rod in the Hardy plant. Here the mandrel is seen on the bench being carefully placed along the edge of the cloth pattern before being mechanically wrapped and rolled. This process is done by lowering the upper portion of the bench to the rolling bed, which then swings across the bed at an angle complementary to the taper of the former, where a simultaneous application of heat causes a bonding to occur as the cloth is rolled around the steel mandrel.

(from an applicational standpoint) made today — although some are much better than others! Buy a rod in the medium or slightly above-medium price range, and you will invariably obtain a very satisfactory piece of fly-fishing equipment.

A brief outline explaining the manufacture of hollow, tapered rod shafts follows. It may be of interest to the reader and provide him with an understanding of the process of production of tapered tubular rod blanks. When rods which are cast single handedly, as opposed to those cast with two hands, are compared, above line Class Seven or Eight (in the A.F.T.M.A. system), tubular-shafted rods are superior to solid-built bamboo rods on a weight/power ratio of assessment.

The material from which most tubular rods is made is glass fiber, which the rod manufacturer receives in the form of a woven cloth, already impregnated with the thermo-plastic compound (the resin). It looks rather like a bale of brownish cotton fabric treated with a coating of glossy starch. Let me emphasize that at this stage in manufacture, it is the quality of the resin and the fineness of the woven material that decide the quality of the finished article.

The cloth is cut to a computerized pattern for the rod length and power, which matches the steel former on to which the cloth will be wrapped. The warp is placed to run up the rod, and the weft strands are around it. The cloth is wrapped a total of three turns around the mandrel. (The steel former has been previously treated with a liquid compound which eliminates any danger of the adhesion of the cloth to the metal former.)

After being wrapped, the mandrel is rolled on a hot bench that provides sufficient heat to make the impregnated cloth tacky, so that it is stuck, each turn to the last. The steel former, with its sticky wrapping of cloth is tightly machine-bound with cellophane strip and is then hung with dozens more in a huge oven. When filled, the doors are sealed, and a computerized clock system takes command. The following is a most critical process: there is a very gradual rise in temperature over a period of several hours, allowing the resin applied to the three turns of cloth to slightly liquify, thoroughly wetting the material but not heating it to a state of viscosity. This condition is held for a certain time, then there is an equal period allotted to a gradual lowering of temperature to ensure a positive bonding, after which the oven is opened, the formers with the fiber glass sheaths are taken out, and the tubular shaft is removed from the mandrel by a mechanical ram. When the curing process and the lamination are satisfactorily completed, the blanks are made smooth by a polishing/grinding process, and then paint-dipped several times, after which they are ready to be made into fishing rods.

Experimentation with new rod materials never ceases and new discoveries in resin types, fibers, and filaments will continue to advance the quality of the tubular product, while new adhesives and developments in the bamboo-rod form — the revival of the five-sided cane rod, for example — will move steadily on.

ROD HANDLES AND REEL FITTINGS

All fly rods are intended to be cast with one hand, with the exception of longer types for salmon angling that are designed to be cast with both hands, an aspect which will be dealt with in another chapter.

Cork has so far not been surpassed by any other material, natural or man-made, from which to make a fly-rod handle. Cork is firm, not warm or

The construction of a cork handle. Shives are fitted individually and, by this method, the one above is ensured of being glued to the one below. Note the board held to the chest of the craftsman which is used to press the corks into place, and the drilled wooden thread bobbin is employed to hold that portion of the blank (which will later receive a screw reel seat) that will be the cork grip section. The jaws of the vice hold a circular block which has a hole drilled in the center through which the upper part of the rod butt is passed. However, the cork shives, being much broader, are in contact with the surface of the block. The craftsman pushes the corks together in the desired position using the board at his chest and the drilled block gripped in the vice.

cold, with a fractional degree of pliability, and a friendly feel in the hand to which rubbery plastics cannot compare. A special champagne-quality cork handle on a fly rod is a joy to behold and a pleasure to use.

Drilled, circular shives, cut from the bark of cork trees, are glued to each other on the rod blank and turned in a lathe to a shape that is comfortable to hold and pleasing to the eye. Most handles are cigar-shaped, and the only advice I have is to avoid too slim a grip, as it tends to give hand cramp after many hours of concentrated fly fishing. The shape of the rod handle is ultimately a matter of personal preference.

The reel seat is situated below the handle of the single-handed fly rod

29

and although there are many variations of reel fitting styles, many immediately recognizable as the product of a particular manufacturer, all perform the same function: they attach the reel securely to the rod. The weight factor of an all-metal screw-lock reel fitting against a single sliding ring and wedge-dome cap cannot of course be ignored. However, this again is mostly a matter of personal choice.

Assorted Reel Fittings and Some of the More Popular Shapes of Fly-Rod Handles

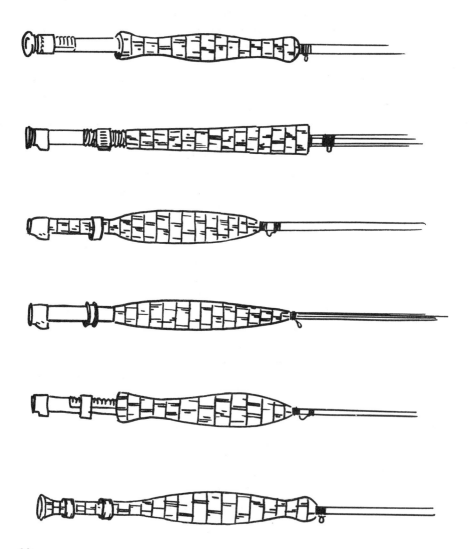

LINE GUIDES

The intermediate line guides used on fly rods are either of the snake type or open-bridge ring style. In both cases the size is graduated on the rod, small at the top to large at the butt of the rod. The end guide is usually a lightweight tube with a hard metal loop. On all quality rods the lowest butt guide is also invariably a hard metal ring. At these two points, the tip and the butt, the guides are subjected to the most frictional wear from the angle of contact of the line passing through them.

Guides are bound to the rod by thread, silk being the material used for the whippings of top-quality rods, while nylon polyester thread is used for the majority of wrappings on mass-produced rods. Silk is a traditional material associated with the evolution of fly rods. However, the use of modern, rot-proof synthetics does not create any mental trauma as far as I am concerned, although my remarks may be classed as Babylonian by some.

Several years ago I was involved with the field testing of a "revolutionary" flexible guide that at first glance appeared to offer advantages over the conventional guides because it was lighter and actually did flex with the rod. On testing, however, the weight of the line pulled the flexible guide to the side near the butt of the rod and, on the backcast, twisted the upper portion of the blank to the rear. This was caused by the pliability of the guide. Needless to say, the guide did not prove of use to the fly fisherman, and acceptance of the snake or bridge, which hold the line close to the fly rod, without being so small as to restrict the flow of the line, is placed firmly in favor of these two types.

LINES

Regardless of situation, in the general angling performance of the fly-fishing outfit, both casting skill and fishing adroitness hinge upon how well the rod and line work together. Ignoring completely how expert the angler may be and how artfully he can cast, unless rod and line are matched on a power/weight basis of assessment, the most satisfactory angling results cannot be achieved nor will the mechanics of casting be efficiently performed.

The line of the fly fisherman is as important as his rod, although a line does not receive, even remotely, the same degree of reverence from the angler. Possibly this is because of the uniformity of the product and its relatively short service life.

A line that is too light in weight for a rod will not allow the angler to assert the full power of the rod (a most frustrating situation) because of insufficient weight to load (flex) the rod: too heavy a line — the lesser of the two evils — will quickly smother the rod by stifling the flex and recoil action, by overloading the power of the rod with too much weight.

When a line develops a very cracked dressing in the tip section after little use, it is a sure sign of a line too light in weight being used on a rod of a more powerful assessment, although a too-fast casting action by the angler may occasionally be the cause. (The repeated snapping off of the fly will serve as confirmation of this fault.)

To cast well, a fly line must be pliable. As a matter of fact, the more inert the material, the better it will cast. Stiffness and wiry line and leader materials are often thought to be the answer to a particular casting problem when, in truth, the solution lies in proper *weight* and *pliability!* The softer and the more supple the line, the more readily it accepts the energizing motion of the casting action of the rod.

The distribution of the weight in the line (remember the fly line is an elongated casting weight) is controlled by the shape of the line, which affects casting performance too. These factors are well known to the manufacturers of quality lines, and are features that are passed on to the angler after experimentation and practical field testing by casting and fishing experts.

Fly-Line Profiles

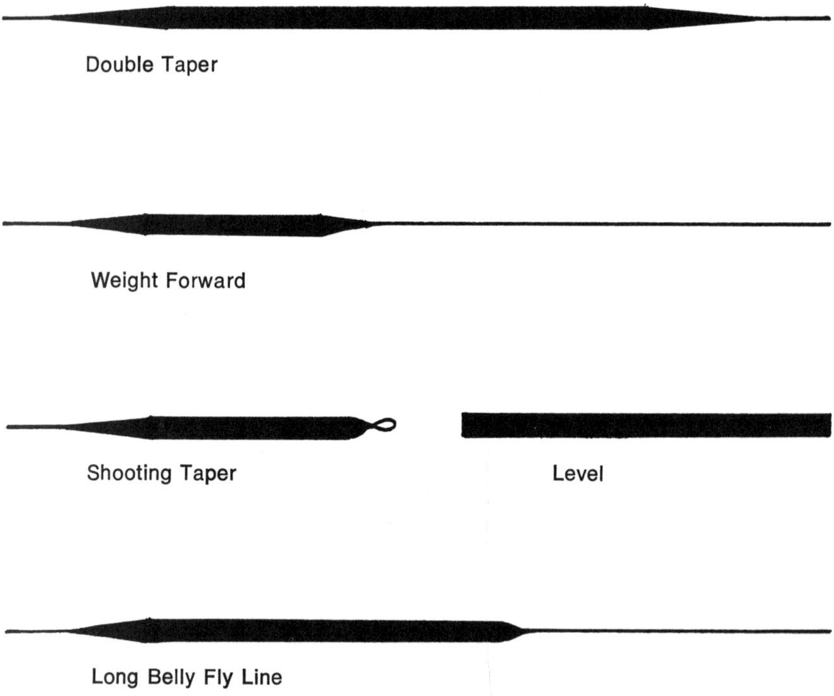

Double Taper

Weight Forward

Shooting Taper   Level

Long Belly Fly Line

Modern fly lines have four basic profiles, although materials, tapers, and finishes vary slightly with every manufacturer. The *level* line is of uniform diameter throughout its complete length and is normally twenty-yards long;

the *double taper* line is usually thirty yards in length and is really a level line with a tapered portion at either end; there is the *weight forward* (Longbelly, Rocket, and Torpedo are all W.F. types) which has the silhouette of a spear, consisting of a tapered section building up to a level portion (the belly of the line) tapering down quickly to the running line at the rear. It measures the same as the D.T. at ninety feet; and finally, the thirty-foot single or *shooting taper* or head that consists of a tapered section leading to a heavier part which is the casting belly. In profile it is rather like a wedge.

Grading the general angling and casting abilities of the floating line in the four basic profiles of fly line, taking into account the fishing values and angling presentational aspects first and the distance casting capability as a secondary consideration, we rate the double taper first, the weight forward second, the level third, and the specialized shooting taper fourth (this line being used solely for maximum distance casting). It should be noted that over line Class Six or Seven, where distance rates over presentation, the weight forward line is more popular with the modern fly fisherman. The sinking tip and intermediate lines are rated in the same order, while the sinking line in the same basic profiles reverses positions One and Two and has an assessment of W.F., D.T., L., and S.T.

Present-day fly lines are manufactured by a process that uses a level, braided line as a core that is covered with a plastic coating. Braided nylon polyester line is the material used for floating lines, and dacron-based braids are used for the production of sinking lines, the former being lighter in weight and more suitable for the manufacture of buoyant lines than the latter, which are heavier and better suited for sinking types. It is the plastic covering, which is a refined and sophisticated form of vinyl coating baked on to the braided core, which decides the quality and purpose of the modern line of the fly fisherman.

It is the specific gravity of the coating of plastic that controls the angling performance of the line and it is the pliability of the material that governs casting efficiency. The plastic covering the core of the floating line contains a fine powdery compound produced by a chemical action that has caused each microscopic particle to take the form of a tiny glass-like hollow sphere — hence the claim by manufacturers that floating fly lines contain millions of air bubbles right into the line. The vinyl covering on the braided core of sinking lines often contains granulated metal to ensure that they sink readily, while other sinking lines have an extremely fine copper wire contained within the braided dacron core. From the foregoing, I trust the reader has a better knowledge of the manufacturing process of modern fly lines, although I may have made an enormously complex production process involving a high degree of technology sound extremely simple.

The taper of the modern fly line is built upon the parellel-braided core, whereas the braided lines of the past had the shape of the line woven into them, an operation which took many days.

The oil-based dressing process that was used for silk lines necessitated that the lines be hung in a tower where they received the numerous oil treatments, repeated soakings and squeezings, rubbings, and polishing that they required. Today's line needs very little care, while the oil-dressed line of yesteryear needed constant attention. Production of braided lines using nylon polyester, dacron, and other fibers with woven tapers were tried, but the chaos of trying to establish the correct weight assessment of the lines, based on the standards set by the silk lines, was unacceptable to the fly fisherman.

The old braided silk lines with their oil-based dressing had to be dried off after each outing to avoid the eventual rotting of the material and to prevent the dressing from turning tacky. They had to be completely removed from the reel at the end of each season and hung in a temperate spot that allowed the air to circulate around them to prevent them from becoming sticky. It was necessary to grease a silk line if it were to be used for dry-fly fishing and had to float. Moreover, it was accepted policy to have two silk lines, a "wet" and a "dry". From my memories of silk, I dimly recall them as lines that would sink when required to float, and when supposed to sink, would cling to the surface with amazing tenacity.

But as a casting line material there is none finer than silk. Pierre Creuse-vaut dominated the European Trout Fly Accuracy scene for years with a silk fly line, which he claimed was slower in the air, and easier to place on the water than plastic materials. His performance in fly accuracy events confirms his statements. In fly-distance casting, the silk tourney lines that won events for Captain Tommy Edwards of Britain, a contemporary of Marvin Hedge of the United States, are still the treasured and used possessions of an envied few of present-day tournament casters.

A silk line has a much smaller diameter than a similar weight of floating line in plastic; a greased silk line floats upon the surface of the water, while the modern plastic line lies in the surface film; the silk line moves more slowly through the air than the vinyl-coated line.

The high-floating silk line when first greased is a joy to use. It lifts from the water like a dream, mends and roll casts beautifully, and casts superbly. However, a silk line that has become water-logged is a diabolical curse. The plastic lines do exactly what they claim to do — float, sink, sink fast, sink extra fast, one part sinks and the rest floats! Occasional washing with mild, soapy lukewarm water will remove dirt which tends to affect the performance of the modern line and, if contact with petrochemical compounds such as gasoline and some fly repellant sprays is avoided, it will give yeoman service, and do it well.

The colors of floating fly lines are normally contained within the lighter shades of the spectrum, which enables the angler to see his line on the surface of the water, and provides a less conspicuous outline image when

(a) The single-action Bogdan

(b) The three-part construction of the Bogdan multiplier showing the excellent engineering work and drag features in these reels.

The "Bogdan," a favorite reel of North American Atlantic salmon anglers, has proved its worth innumerable times on Canadian rivers.

---

viewed from below. The sinking lines are invariably in darker tones of green and brown blending easily into the surroundings found below the surface. Sink-float lines are two-tone; a dark color for the sinking portion and a light for the floating section.

I recall my early fishing days, when, being the proud possessor of a level Number One silk line, a gift for my eleventh birthday, I would fish dry fly with it until it sank, which was the signal to switch to a wet fly or sit and wait for the line to dry. The decision whether to keep fishing or "dry-off" and hope there would be a hatch of flies later, certainly made one evaluate the angling situation a great deal more closely than is done today.

Tapered silk lines coated with a modern synthetic dressing are once more available to the fly fisherman at roughly twice the price of a top quality plastic line. These will appeal to a small section of the fly-fishing population but will not be the choice of most anglers, who favor the modern plastic fly line because it is available in such a wide range of densities for so many varied angling applications.

The present-day plastic line is the product of modern technology, a supreme example of a blend of the old and new. The new materials have opened up new areas of fly-fishing interest, added new horizons to the sport, and created vastly greater dimensions to the world of fly fishing.

A craftsman in Alnwick checking the fitting of the handle to the line spool of a Hardy "Marquis" fly reel. This is only one of many inspections associated with the production of any top-quality tackle and, although adding to the cost, ensures that the angler will receive a perfect item of equipment.

REELS

The reel is an item of equipment that is assessed by the fly-casting population, from a lowly position of being simply a part of the outfit, to the other extreme, where it plays a role of the utmost angling importance.

There is a simple explanation for these variances of opinion: the type of angling situation, and the quality of the fishing. For example, if the fish are small and the stream is narrow, it is most unlikely that a fish will ever take line from the reel. In such a circumstance the reel could well be treated as "the part of the tackle where the line is stored." However, when the fish are large, and the line is taken from the reel on the strike and there is the strong likelihood of the fish making long runs after being hooked, the reel becomes a most essential part of the outfit.

As a rule, the fly reel consists of three main parts — the reel saddle, known also as the seat or foot; the cage or frame; and the drum or spool.

36

Inside the frame is situated the spindle and ratchet system. There is some-times a line guard fitted to the outer surface of the cage to prevent the line from wearing a groove in the metal of the frame.

It is generally single action (a one-to-one ratio of line recovery to the turn of the handle). It has a fixed ratchet, sometimes called the click or check mechanism, which is there primarily to eliminate line over-run when line is stripped by hand from the reel by the angler during casting or while being speedily taken by a running fish — the spool a blur of motion, accom-panied by the reassuring purr of the ratchet as it controls the spinning-line drum.

Some better-quality fly reels have an adjustment screw which alters the pressure of the check mechanism — really a simple drag tension — that is intended to be varied according to the strength of the leader being used, and actually enables the fly fisherman to tune his tackle to a finer degree than can be achieved with the fixed check.

The click mechanism is normally a triangular pawl (metal wedge), anchored in the reel frame, that is kept in contact with a gear wheel on the inside of the line drum by a metal spring pressing on the base of the pawl and forcing the apex of the triangular check into the gear wheel of the spool as it turns around the spindle of the reel which is located in the center of the frame. Another form of check mechanism is a spring stud situated on the internal face of the reel drum which is pressed into contact with an indented recessed circular track located at the base of the spindle when the spool is fitted into the cage.

Line spools of the modern fly reel can be easily detached, locking with a spring lever on to the grooved head of the spindle (unlike the reels of yester-year that were screw-bolted together and in some cases unable to be taken apart at all). This feature of speedy drum removal encourages anglers to carry extra spools, loaded with various types of lines, which enables them to adapt to prevailing angling conditions without having to carry several reels.

Some line spools have a flange which is situated outside the cage (the majority are contained within the frame). This design allows the angler to control a fish by finger control upon the exposed flange, a feature that may occasionally be of use to the average angler, although most fishermen control the line by finger pressure exerted inside the drum from below, when the circumstances demand it.

A fly reel is a piece of equipment that has advanced to a place of im-portance from the much lower area of prominence it occupied in the olden days, when it first was a wooden bobbin large enough to store the braided horse hair line, and later became a metal winch that not only stored the line but also helped counterbalance the long unwieldy rods, before moving gradually to the stage of mechanical efficiency, excellence of design, and angling proficiency, produced in lightweight metal, that is available today.

One of the finest custom-made reels available and one which enjoys the full acceptance of the most discriminating North American fly fishermen, the "Walker," produced by Arthur L. Walker and Son Inc.

During the course of tackle advancement, there was for a while an accepted method of fly reel selection that has gradually disappeared as fly rods have become more efficient casting tools, and the development of lines to perform specific angling duties was realized. This was the system whereby a heavy reel was matched to a rod where the rod tip was held high — dry fly; and a lightweight reel was fitted to a rod that was held low to the water — wet fly, and was an aspect of the old balance theory that no longer is applied to modern fly-fishing equipment, balance today being the terminology for pairing the correct weight of line to a rod of similar casting power.

There are many types of fly reels available to the fly fisherman, all of which are attached to the rod, behind the hand, and hang below the rod. They can be separated into three categories: the standard single action, the multiplier (geared for faster line recovery) and the automatic, a reel which has a wind-up spring mechanism activated when the line is stripped from the reel and which, when a lever that controls the spring is moved, recovers the line.

The first type is by far the most popular, representing possibly 95% of the complete fly-fishing reel market. The second type offers a faster rate of recovery of line — an advantage that a vast majority of anglers do not find necessary. The third type has two disadvantages to be weighed against the

Tycoon Fin-Nor reels are renowned for their efficiency and superb engineering. Many experts consider them the best big-game fly-reels for either salt or fresh water.

clock-work line recovery feature. These are a very definite "overweight" problem (it being double that of the single action), and a lack of space for any appreciable amount of backing line.

Filling a reel with backing line beneath the main line serves two purposes: there is a reserve quantity of line to rely upon should a large fish be hooked and decide to move off-shore or swim downstream, and, there is the fact that a filled spool utilizes the largest amount of the circumference of the spool of the reel to provide a speedy recovery of line.

A couple of decades ago reels and the drums with which they were fitted were produced with either narrow, medium, or wide spools made for angling for small, middle-sized, and large fish. Today the width of most reels is narrow to medium, and with larger diameters than those of the past. The choice of size is governed by the line type and the backing it must hold. All types and makes of fly reels have their advocates and selecting from single action, multiplier, and automatic reels is really a matter of personal choice.

There is, of course, the question of which hand should operate the reel. Should the dominant hand that casts the rod do only that, allowing the secondary hand to strip the line from the reel and also to recover the line, or, is it permissable to change hands? Quite frankly, I discover no inconvenience in casting and then placing the rod in the secondary hand to recover line. I suggest the angler use the method which suits him best.

Reels by Hardy Brothers of England are noted for both their elegance and excellence, while the efficiency of the beautiful custom-made Walker range of fly reels represents a pinnacle of the American reel makers' art. The superb drag adjustments of the magnificent handcrafted Bogdan and Fin Nor reels are recognized as the finest available when tarpon, bonefish, and salmon are encountered.

The perforated drum of certain makes was originally there to allow air to reach oil-dressed lines. Today, however, its only purpose is to reduce reel weight and perhaps also to enhance its appearance.

My advice is: always buy a reel of comparable value to the rest of your equipment, for it is the functional efficiency of the reel that will ultimately decide whether the fish of a lifetime will be landed or lost. Just as an athlete uses his reserves of energy and his store of strength to win a competition, so the fly reel holds a reserve of line and adds its strength to the power of a rod to land a fish. A fly reel should be mechanically sound, of good functional design, and large enough to hold the line and backing necessary for the chosen form of angling.

I prefer a narrow, lightweight single-action fly reel. It is once again a personal preference, for when aesthetics and other individual values such as design, color, and size are taken into consideration, one appreciates how individual a fly fishing outfit can be.

LEADERS

The modern tapered leader, knotless from the heavy butt to the fine tippet, is a tremendous improvement over the silkworm "gut" leaders that were knotted every sixteen inches, this being the maximum stretch available in silkworm gut. This material had to be soaked before use and was prone to rot, yet it, in turn, had proved vastly superior to the hair from the tail of a stallion (as opposed to strands from the female of the species which contained a certain amount of ammonia and was therefore not so strong).

Tapered nylon monofilament knotless leaders are extruded in a continuous stream from a molten compound, slightly cooled, stretched to the profile required, then heated and stretched once more to align the molecules of the substance to add greater strength, control the elasticity of the material, and provide a higher degree of finish to the surface of the leader. Nylon is not as heavy as gut, which consequently cast much better than monofilament, as any old-time angler will verify.

One measurement of leader identification dating back to the days of silkworm gut still persists. This is the "X" rating of leader diameter, a system which is translated for the present-day fly fisherman:

X Rating Drawn Gut	Diameter in MM one hundredths of a millimeter	Diameter in Inches one thousandths of an inch	Approximate Pounds Test in Monofilament
0	26	.011	10
1	24	.010	8
2	22	.009	6
3	18	.008	5
4	16	.007	4
5	15	.006	3
6	14	.005	2
7	12	.004	1

There are an appreciable number of fly fishermen who make up their own leaders from small ten-yard coils of monofilament, produced specifically for this purpose. They build the tapers of the leader by knotting varying diameters of nylon. Possibly the most-used formula for leader construction is the one by McClane of 60% weight, 20% taper, and 20% tippet (which in a simple conversion is six feet made from stout nylon, two feet of sections which taper steadily from the thick material to the final two feet of fine tippet lengths).

I prefer to use the continuous taper, knotless type and, when additional length is needed, add either a heavier section above or attach a lighter strength tippet piece to the fine end, or, occasionally do both.

The main disadvantage of knotted leaders becomes apparent when thread weeds and algae are abundant. Each knot collects pieces of the floating plant life, and after a few casts the leader looks like a necklace of green beads with each knot wrapped with weed or enveloped in a ball of algae.

Great faith and work are put into leader design and leader building by a sizable number of anglers in order to obtain fly turnover and leader extension. However, it is the correct delivery of the forward cast that plays a more important role. Having dared to say this, I do not wish the statement to be misconstrued, as leader taper does aid casting and presentational ability, but unless the line is cast correctly, the best-designed leader in the world cannot produce a miracle of placement.

CHAPTER 3

Choosing Fly-Fishing Tackle

Impregnated slivers of bamboo, fiber cloth, or strands of other filaments and thermo-plastic resins that provide the basis of the modern fly rod; the mechanical perfection of finely-tooled light-weight fly reels; scientifically produced lines with polyvinyl coatings; knotless, tapered extruded monofilament leaders; the best quality eyed steel hooks, and flies made from the finest of synthetic and natural materials, are all at the disposal of the present-day fly fisherman.

Selection of fly-fishing equipment in Walton's day based rod length on river width and line to rod length. Yet even then lines were tapered by a system of adding an extra strand of horse hair to each link as the line was built up towards the junction with the tip of the rod, where it was whipped to the end of the top section. The strength of the leader section consisted of two hairs, to the hook, and was judged by Cotton as sufficient to kill a twenty-inch trout!

I remember reading as a boy an old angling book (alas, discarded in my youth as obsolete!) which gave this piece of information as a guide to rod selection: "When the rod be held parallel to the water it should dip not not more than two feet twixt tip and butt." This referred to rods of eighteen feet, in four sections. The lower two sections were hollowed out by a hot wire-burning process, and weighed roughly 1½ ounces per foot!

The selection of present-day fly fishing equipment is best based initially on what is to be cast (the size of fly), then how big the fish are that the angler expects to catch and, finally, where it will be used. What is to be cast rather than what is to be caught, before where it will be used. Once this theory is accepted, the choice of suitable fly fishing equipment is made easy. Each power assessment contained within the A.F.T.M.A. system has a clearly-defined performance area, governed by the combined line weight and rod power which controls angling potential, and informs the angler of the casting capabilities and the angling application of the fly-fishing outfit.

The A.F.T.M.A. numerical system of tackle assessment contained between Numbers 3 and 12 can be separated into three operational zones, three,

42

A selection of modern fly-fishing equipment.

4 and 5 being classifications that provide exceptionally "light" and delicate fly presentation using small flies and supply the maximum of sport when a fish is hooked. Six, 7, 8 are intermediate powers and are normally embraced within a "basic" category and contribute a higher degree of "positive" line control, lacking however the capabilities of lightness of presentation of the outfits in the first grouping, yet possessing greater angling power in both casting ability and handling the average sizes of flies, together with the mastery of a hooked fish because of the "stronger" classification. Nine, 10, 11, and 12 are the "powerhouse" division of the A.F.T.M.A. rating. They are capable of casting farther and throwing larger flies than the others, and truly have the power to dominate the quarry of the fly-fishing angler.

My statement "what is to be cast, rather than what is to be the catch" may now perhaps have greater meaning if we continue to view the fly-fishing outfit first as a casting implement and then as angling equipment, and use the A.F.T.M.A. classification as the basis of explanation.

The line, regardless of density and profile, or whether it is floating, sinking or sink-float, level, double taper, weightforward or shooting taper, conforms to the weight system upon which the A.F.T.M.A. number is based, while the rod bears a similar numerical designation, which is the manufacturer's power rating.

Since 1960, when the system was devised, the casting potential of fly-fishing equipment has been refined, the angling application of the tackle still further rationalized, and fishing technique has become much more sophisticated. However, the fundamentals remain the same — a line of a specific weight is cast by a rod of a similar relative power: the line mass is being pushed and pulled through the air as efficiently as the rod — and the ability of the angler — will allow; the line weight and form is pushing and pulling an optimum size of fly attached to a leader, back and forth, and is presenting it to the water (the fish) as effectively and precisely as possible.

The pertinent phrases contained in the last paragraph require still greater emphasis, for they are the root from which stems the rudiments of good casting and better presentation, together with superior fly-fishing performance. Remember always that the line is the weight that is cast by the rod and that the fly, tied to a leader attached to the line, is pulled back and forth by the rod, giving motion to the line, and that leader and fly contribute nothing other than resistance to the movement. There is, under these conditions of casting, an optimum size of fly, relative to line class and rod power for maximum fly-fishing efficiency.

Relationship of Fly-Fishing Classification to Hook Size and Average Angling Operation (Casting/Fishing Distance)

A.F.T.M.A. Ratings	Hook Size	Angling Operation in feet
3	16—28	5—35
4	12—22	5—45
5	10—18	10—55
6	6—16	10—65
7	2—14	15—75
8	1/0—12	15—80
9	2/0—6	20—85
10	3/0—4	20—95
11	4/0—1	25—90
12	5/0—1/0	25—80

To give this statement still more significance, let us apply the theory to a more readily understood area of angling: spinning. A tiny lure is not normally attached to an extremely strong line and used on a powerful two-handed rod, nor would a huge spinning lure be tied to an exceptionally fine line and cast with a lightweight rod. In the casting of a fly the same rules apply. The average size of fly to be cast should decide to a very great extent the test of the leader, weight of line, and the power of rod.

Just as the size of a natural bait, such as a worm, a grain of corn, a tiny squid or a minnow, decides the size of the hook to be used (and not the size of the fish it is expected to catch — only the strength of the iron being the primary consideration) so the size of the fly to be cast determines to a very great extent the rod power and the line weight of the fly-fishing outfit.

Naturally there are other considerations to be taken into account, such as prevalent winds, overgrown streams, very wide rivers, snag-filled ponds and weedy lakes. However, the average size of fly to be cast is the basis of fly-tackle selection before all else.

The rod, being both a lever and a spring, imparts movement to the elongated weight, the line, by the casting action which is the method of propulsion. It is the speed, the velocity transmitted — in a controlled way, not violently, to the line by the rod that governs how well a cast is executed.

It is interesting to note at this stage that the cast of the angler requires the line to reverse its mass as it unfurls back and forth, and the more inert the material, the more supple, pliable, and soft the weave and dressing from which the line is made, the more readily and better will it perform this function.

The subject of casting, from the standpoint of the transmission of movement to the line by the rod, is contained within the realms of kinetic energy. A later section deals with the matter in more depth. It is a subject which at this stage can be totally disregarded, to be mulled over some evening during the closed season in connection with the fly-fishing angler's cast.

A rod of specific power (the casting tool) is only capable of generating a certain amount of energy to the line (the casting weight). The line, in turn, on the acceptance of movement, has a limited ability as to what it can pull through the air (the fly). The feathered hook attached to a leader can be progressed to a size that offers maximum resistance to the air until it reaches a point which a line cannot efficiently carry or place on to the water for optimum angling proficiency. In plain terms, this means that there are certain sizes of fly that are best cast from specific rod powers and line weights. There are limits to the size of fly a rod and line can throw and, although there is no limitation as to how small a fly may be used, tiny flies are invariably used in conjunction with light-line outfits that provide delicate placement and gentle fly presentation.

The fishing fly is a suggestive, imitative, attractive, irritating, simulative, stimulative, many-formed, multi-hued arrangement of feathers, tinsel, and fur tied with silk to a hook which, in turn, can be either up eyed or down, either long shank, normal, or short, made from round or flattened (forged) wire.

The anatomy of a hook consists of an eye, shank, bend, and barb. The distance between the point of the barb and the shank is the gape, and the space contained behind this place of measurement is the throat of the hook.

It is scarcely possible to believe that even today there is no standardization of hook size, the method of gauge being based upon the length of the shank excluding the eye (a system dating back to the early days of the industry in Redditch when a hook was first a needle). As hook patterns vary greatly, the only true assessment of a particular hook size is by visual appreciation.

A fly is made to represent — perhaps suggest or infer are more honest words — the food upon which the species that is angled for feed. Or, it is dressed in a combination of colors or styles that will prove attractive enough to induce the fish to take it, or irritate it sufficiently to provoke an attack. No matter what the stimulus, all provide the "strike" at the submerged fly and the "rise" to a floating pattern.

The size and coloration of the feathered lure are normally close to that which it attempts to suggest or resemble: a small crustacean; a tiny insect larva or pupa; any of the innumerable underwater denizens; smaller fishes; floating insects; frogs; terrestials such as ants, grasshoppers, and mice.

Tackle selection should be based on the size of the fly to be cast and fished with and then on the physical angling situation. This is the only sound procedure to adopt when choosing fly-fishing equipment.

Table Showing the Suitability and Selection of Fly-Fishing Equipment Based on the Method of Appropriate Hook Size, Species of Fish, Average Rod Length, and the A.F.T.M.A. Rating of Lines and Rods with Areas of Maximum Angling Application Detailed

A.F.T.M.A. Line Classification	Hook Size	Rod Length	A.F.T.M.A. Rod Classification		
3	16-28	5½'-6½'	Pan Fish Perch	3 4 5 / 4 5 6 / 5 6 7 / 6 7 8	Trout Grayling
4	12-22	6'-7'			
5	10-18	7'-7½'			
6	6-16	7½'-8½'			
7	2-14	7½'-8½'	Mackerel	7 8 9 / 8 9 10	Bass
8	1/0-12	8'-9'			
9	2/0-6	8½'-9½'	Pike Walleye Pickerel	9 10 11 / 10 11 12	Salmon
10	3/0-4	9'-10'			
11	4/0-1	9'-9½'	Saltwater Muskie	11 12 / 12	
12	5/0-1/0	9'-9½'			

A Guide for Leader Tippet Strength for Hook Size:

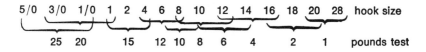

5/0	3/0	1/0	1	2	4	6	8	10	12	14	16	18	20	28	hook size
	25	20		15		12	10	8	6		4		2	1	pounds test

For most fly fishermen the first choice will probably be selected from the "basic" tackle in what can be described as Zone Two of the A.F.T.M.A. classification, although of course there will be occasions when an outfit in Zone One, the "presentational" strengths, or Zone Three, the "power-houses," are chosen, the choice depending on what has to be cast, where, and at which species.

Perhaps a word of advice concerning the inevitable accumulation of fly-fishing outfits is worth passing on. The fisherman would be wise to amass his fly-fishing tackle on a basis of even, (4, 6, 8, 10, 12) or odd, (3, 5, 7, 9, 11) rather than on a consecutive basis — initially! An odd or even selection, blanketing a particular species, offers a more versatile angling equipment arsenal than two rods immediately next to each other in power ratings.

For example, for trout fishing, a Number 6, for streamers and wet flies; a Number 4 for nymphs and dry flies; and a Number 8 where wind, larger flies, perhaps longer casts and bigger fish are to be encountered. For summer salmon a Number 8 for the small and medium flies; and a Number 10 for the larger flies cast in the spring and the bulky dry flies used during the summer months. A Number 7 and Number 9 for the various sizes of flies used for walleye, pickerel, and pike and the angling conditions where they

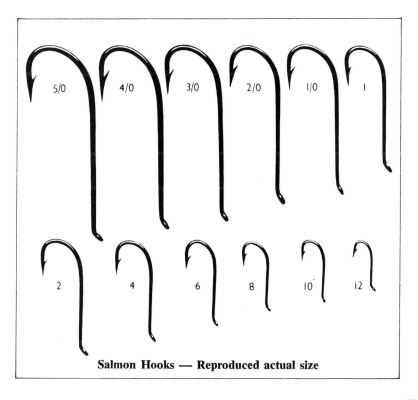

Salmon Hooks — Reproduced actual size

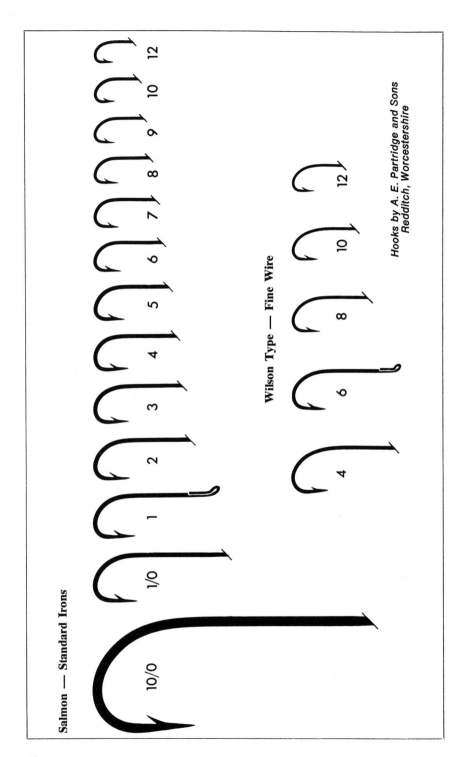

Salmon — Standard Irons

Wilson Type — Fine Wire

Hooks by A. E. Partridge and Sons
Redditch, Worcestershire

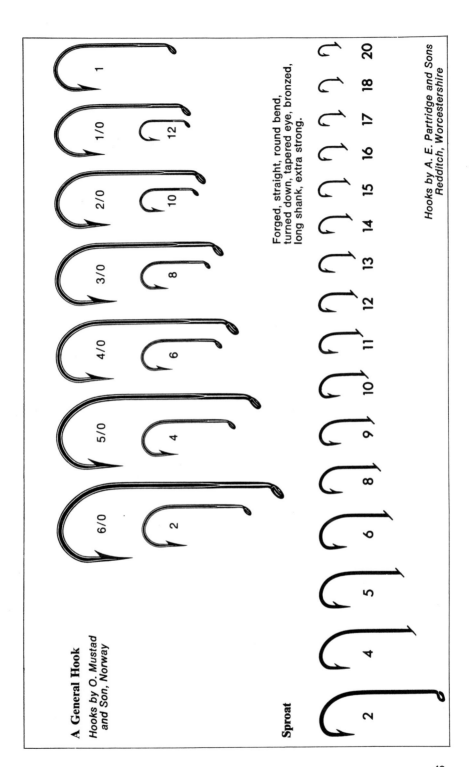

A General Hook
Hooks by O. Mustad and Son, Norway

Sproat

Forged, straight, round bend, turned down, tapered eye, bronzed, long shank, extra strong.

Hooks by A. E. Partridge and Sons Redditch, Worcestershire

49

are caught. A Number 3 and Number 5 to be used on a tiny stream, heavily wooded perhaps, yet capable of providing great sport with small fish, or in a situation that creates demanding angling conditions, cautious fish and crystal clear water, and dictates the use of light tackle before any degree of success can be achieved.

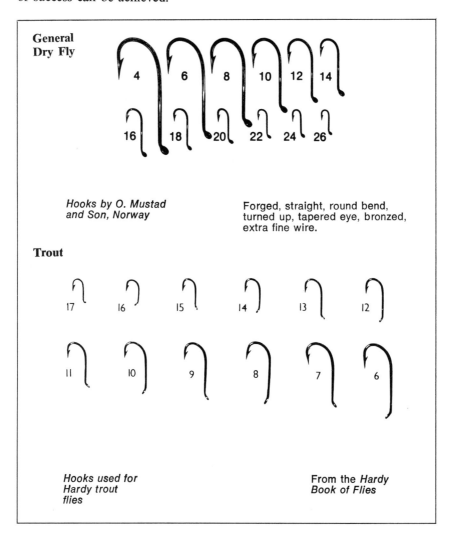

General Dry Fly

Hooks by O. Mustad and Son, Norway

Forged, straight, round bend, turned up, tapered eye, bronzed, extra fine wire.

Trout

Hooks used for Hardy trout flies

From the *Hardy Book of Flies*

TYPES OF FEATHERED LURES

The feathered lure used by the fly fisherman is tied in various forms, dressed in innumerable patterns, and comes in many sizes on numerous types of hooks. All relate to the size, color, and shape of the food form or, are attractors the dimensions of which are relative to the species being angled for. A Leonard Wright #14 caddis imitation, a principal food of trout, would not be used for tarpon, nor would a #5/0, five-inch red and yellow tarpon fly (the Palola Worm) developed by Stu Apte, be used for trout.

Flies can be separated into easily recognizable types. Flies which float, dry flies, represent insects that sit upon the surface of the water, while those which are fished below the surface, wet flies, suggest underwater creatures or insects on the emergent journey they have to make from the bed of the stream or lake to the surface. Streamer flies are very sketchy bait-fish or leech imitations. Other types impersonate with feathers and hair, eels, shrimps, and crayfish. Nymphs are tied to simulate certain types of aquatic life forms. There are also copies of amphibians, floating styles of flies, Bugs which often have bodies made from cork, deer's hair, or balsa wood, dressed to mimic frogs, tadpoles, newts, and salamanders. Ants, beetles, crickets, mice, and grasshoppers are the bases of other floating efforts — Terrestials.

BACKING LINE

It is normal to add backing line either braided bait-casting or squidding, which is fitted to the fly reel before the fly line.

For smaller fish, twenty-five yards of reserve line behind a ninety-foot length of fly line is sufficient. Atlantic salmon fishing requires a minimum of one-hundred yards of backing, while Pacific salmon types are more happily pursued with one-hundred-and-fifty yards of reserve line. Two-hundred yards is the right length for salt-water fly casting for tarpon.

Note that the braided reserve of line must never be of a weaker poundage than the breaking strain of the leader tippet, or the fly caster may create a situation whereby a very large fish making an extra long run may be lost and, instead of departing with only a fly, may take along with it the leader, fly line, and backing.

Floating lines are mostly light in color, touching all tones of white, blue, and green. If dark backing is used there is often an electro-chemical exchange of color shade from the darker to the lighter material which explains the reason for this slight color transfer, and has no detrimental effect on the fly line, leaving only a slight discoloration on the line. This chemical action does not matter if the line is weight forward. As the discoloration is only on the running line, it becomes noticeable when a level or double-tapered line is reversed.

I know a few anglers who use brown, yellow, and green felt-tip pens to "camouflage" the first 10 or 12 feet of the fly line, and claim they have better angling results. This is an area in which I personally have not experimented and I leave this aspect of specialization with the reader for consideration.

Fly Types

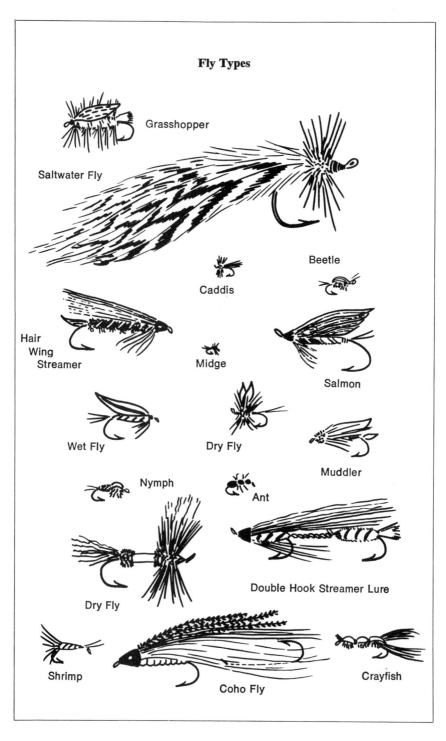

Grasshopper

Saltwater Fly

Beetle

Caddis

Hair Wing Streamer

Midge

Salmon

Wet Fly

Dry Fly

Muddler

Nymph

Ant

Dry Fly

Double Hook Streamer Lure

Shrimp

Coho Fly

Crayfish

Fly Types

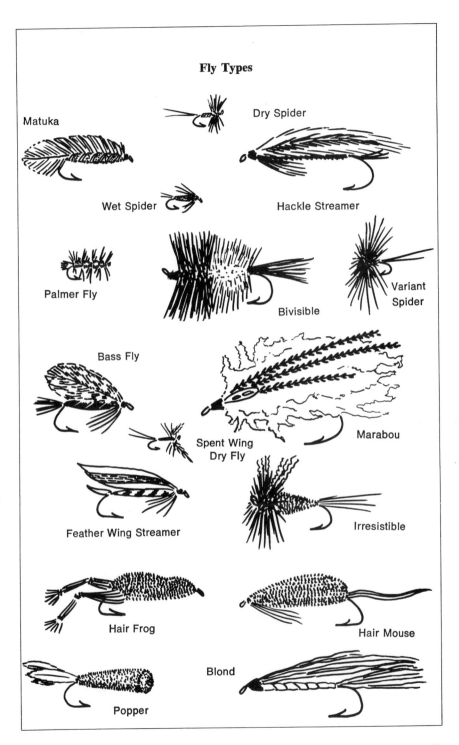

Matuka

Dry Spider

Wet Spider

Hackle Streamer

Palmer Fly

Bivisible

Variant Spider

Bass Fly

Spent Wing Dry Fly

Marabou

Feather Wing Streamer

Irresistible

Hair Frog

Hair Mouse

Popper

Blond

KNOTS

Let us assume the selection of basic equipment has been made, based on what has been outlined, and reference made to the tables which give the rudimentary guidance on tackle ability and angling application — a rod of suitable length and power, and a line for a specific purpose (double taper or weight forward, floating or sinking) of relative weight to the rod power, together with a reel of adequate size (capacity), function, and quality, along with flies, and leaders, all chosen for a specific type of fishing.

Backing line must be fitted to the reel. The fly line must be joined to the backing in a manner that will allow the join to run smoothly through the rod guides, and provide an absolutely secure connection, the leader must be attached to the line tip, and the fly tied to the leader tippet. There are many knots available to the angler for these tasks and the following selection is well tried and proven. They are the most popular knots used by fly fishermen.

Fisherman's Slip Knot — for attaching line to reel spool.

Blood Knot — joining two sections of line, and making a fly dropper.

Blood Knot Variation — used when two lines of unequal thickness are to be joined or when a shock leader is to be fitted for pike or tarpon fishing.

Fisherman's Knot — making a dropper or joining two sections of line.

Shock Leader Knot — joining unequal diameters of monofilament

Leader Loop Knot — the easiest and strongest knot for loop making.

Tucked Clinch Knot — for attaching fly to leader.

Turle Knot — fly to leader.

Snell Knot — making leader links, and attaching large flies to a leader.

Whipping Splice — joining fly line to backing.

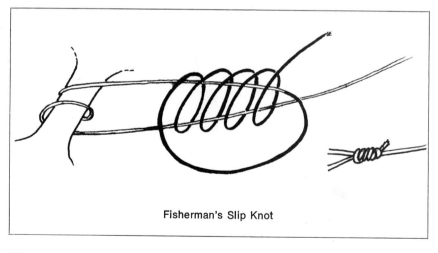

Fisherman's Slip Knot

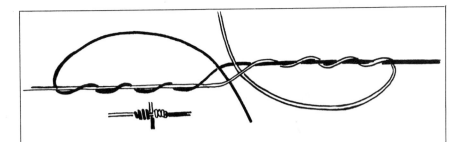

Blood Knot

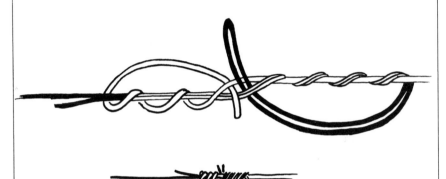

Blood Knot Variation

Used when a rather fine line is joined to a much stouter section.

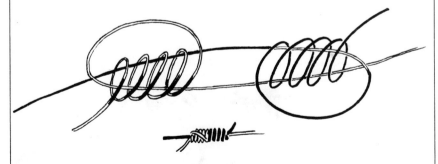

The Fisherman's Knot

This is a very easy knot to tie, and is invaluable when a knot must be tied quickly or in poor light. It also serves very well should a dropper be needed to attach another fly.

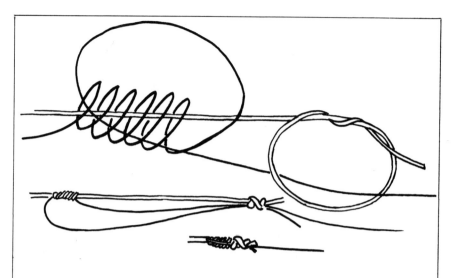

Shock Leader Knot

Used if, for example, 8 pounds and 80-pounds test must be joined for a leader.

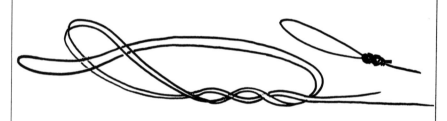

Leader Loop Knot

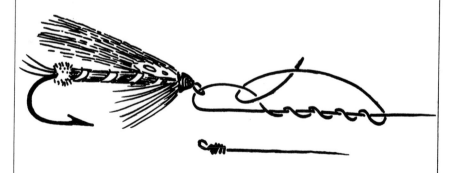

Tucked Clinch Knot

A quickly tied knot, which is very efficient. It is the method of attaching a fly in a poor light.

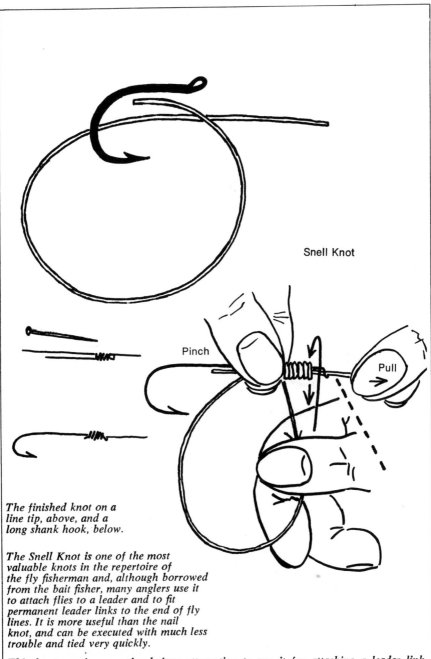

Snell Knot

Pinch

Pull

The finished knot on a
line tip, above, and a
long shank hook, below.

The Snell Knot is one of the most
valuable knots in the repertoire of
the fly fisherman and, although borrowed
from the bait fisher, many anglers use it
to attach flies to a leader and to fit
permanent leader links to the end of fly
lines. It is more useful than the nail
knot, and can be executed with much less
trouble and tied very quickly.

This knot requires practice before attempting to use it for attaching a leader link,
best done on a long shank hook with 15-pounds test nylon. A pin used to provide
rigidity to the fly line tip will assist the forming of the knot, the pin being withdrawn
as the knot is tightened.

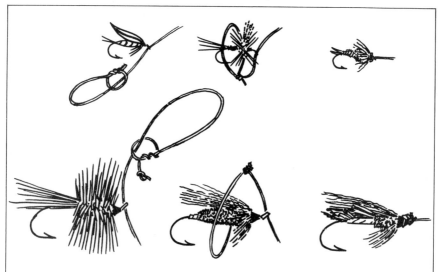

Turle Knot

This knot fastening eliminates any articulation that can occur when the leader is tied directly to the eye of the hook, and is the favored knot of the salmon angler.

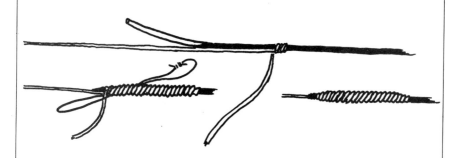

Whipping Splice Knot

The fly line must be anchored securely before this knot can be tied. Wrap the backing down the line, over itself, starting at a point three or four inches up the line. The overall length of the whipping should be about one-inch long. Two-thirds of the wrap being done, a circular loop of strong monofilament should be positioned to pull back the end of the wrapping material to create a whip finish.

After the whipping has been accomplished, both ends of the backing line should be pulled firmly tight, the lines trimmed; the backing cut off close to the point where it protrudes from the splice, and the fly line cut at an acute angle, wrapped with thread, and varnished. This knot, tied as described, will pass smoothly through the line guides and will not come undone as any tension on the lines only serves to pull the whipping tighter. The secret in tying this knot is to keep tension only on the fly line and not the backing when pulling the splice tight. It can be done with as little as four turns, the first two holding, the next two gripping the splice. A length of one inch is better.

There are two usual methods of joining the fly line to the backing which, I would stress, should be a braided line. Monofilament is not to be recommended for this purpose as it can be cut by some obstruction with a sharp edge — coral in salt water and granite in streams and lakes are good examples of natural hazards. There is scarcely a piece of water anywhere in the world that does not contain discarded metal debris. The elasticity of monofilament, reeled on to a line spool under tension (playing a large fish for example) can badly damage a fly reel and, in some cases, burst a line drum.

A specialist dealer will normally provide the service of fitting line and backing to the reel when the equipment is obtained and, either bind the two lines together with thread — a task best left to the expert, or, use the actual backing line to form a whipped attachment join, which is done by wrapping the backing line tightly back over itself and finishing off the wrap with a whip finish. This is the method of line joining which is illustrated. It will prove of the most use to anglers. It is an absolutely safe procedure of attaching braided backing line to the fly line and, when done correctly, any tension applied to the whipping only serves to pull the wrap tighter, which bites deeper into the surface of the line.

When tying knots with monofilament, remember that a maximum of six and a minimum of three turns is a good rule to follow. Always draw the two sections or the single strand, as the case may be, slowly into the knot to ensure even tension and snug the turns evenly. Finish off by giving a firm pull to check the holding power of the knot and then trim off the loose ends. In knot tying, as in anything else, it is a case of practice making perfect.

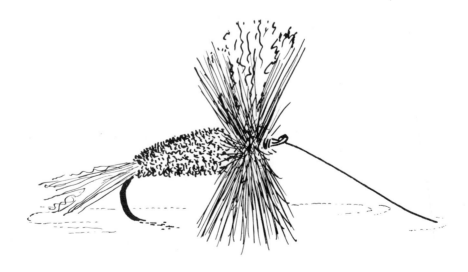

CHAPTER 4

Casting

THE LATERAL TUITION SYSTEM

Learning to cast a fly with modern fly-fishing equipment is relatively easy, once there is a clear understanding of what has to be done and how. Invariably the newcomer experiences some confusion and frustration caused by an image of the classic scene retained in the mind's eye of an angler clearly silhouetted in some idyllic setting, the line flowing to front and rear, the arm moving smoothly back and forth, and the line being laid gently and precisely on to the water in a delightful, effortless, fluid, rhythmic, and graceful casting motion.

Before this stage of casting accomplishment can be reached, there is naturally a fair amount of practice involved, and some measure of angling experience must be accumulated. Accepting this fact, the casting of a fly is not difficult and I would say that within an hour of first placing a balanced fly-fishing outfit into the hand of a person completely new to angling, he will be casting a line well enough to catch a fish, by using the procedures outlined below.

You will recall that initially a fly rod performs both as a lever and a spring and that the fly line, when cast, functions as an elongated weight. The rod when manipulated in the casting action produces subtle, pliant, pushing, and pulling motions which cause compressional flex, together with recoil speed and decompressional thrust. The kinetic impulse transferred to the pliable line, as it accepts the energy of movement, causes it to roll and unfurl with supple ease to the front and rear.

The fundamentals are movement and timing: the basic mechanics of casting are correct power application contained within the visual arm motion, while making allowance for the line to extend fully to the front and rear before changing directions. Synchronizing the rod movement to the speed of the line, within the limits of line travel and airborne placement (the rod being used to push and pull the line, leader, and fly through the air in a back-and-forth motion) before being finally placed upon the water is imperative.

It is not essential to visit a river or lake in order to learn how to cast with a fly-fishing outfit — some of the most successful casting clubs operate in North America during the winter months in school gymnasiums. Any space that allows sufficient area for the line to fully extend to its maximum casting length in both directions, with the caster positioned midway, is all that is required. Select a spot when practising out-of-doors that does not have overhead obstructions such as telephone wires, tree branches, or power cables, and in a school hall avoid basketball nets and dangling ropes.

Jim Hardy, a former World Casting Champion, and a third-generation member of the Hardy Brothers Fishing Tackle Company of Alnwick, is an excellent casting instructor. He always emphasizes the fact that without a correct backcast a good forward delivery of the line cannot be executed. With this wrinkle of knowledge, remember that the distance being cast to the front is also necessary at the rear, in order that the line may extend fully on the backcast without contact with obstructions and that it can be drawn forward cleanly for a good frontal delivery.

A suitable practice area is not too difficult to find. Let us assume we are there, the rod is assembled, the reel is attached to the rod, and the line is threaded through the guides with a leader tied to the tip of the line, and a small piece of wool knotted to the leader tippet to represent the fly.

First, there is a correct way to grip the handle. Holding the rod parallel to the ground with the reel and line guides below, the casting hand should grasp the handle where the contour of the cork offers the most comfortable fit, as if the hand were holding the shank of a hammer.

This hold is undoubtedly the best of all grips. Other variations tend to be restrictive, although grips such as placing the thumb directly on the top of the handle or laying the forefinger along the handle top, do have their advocates. The grip first described (occasionally with the thumb on top) is the one which is invariably chosen by tournament casters where the ultimate in performance is demanded.

Pull line approximately twice the length of rod from the reel and the instruction can begin.

The pupil should stand on the midway point of the narrow rectangular area necessary to cast the line, with an equal distance to the left as to the right, with the wind, if any, blowing from the rear, and gripping the rod as instructed, with the forefinger trapping the line from the reel to the handle.

By a lateral waving action of the rod (achieved by a forearm and wrist movement) the pupil should aerialize the line. Pushing it first to one side then the other — not allowing the line to drop and touch the ground — the object being to have the caster follow the course of the line by watching its progress through the air. The rod-waving motion is done without twisting the wrist and the palm of the hand holding the rod is kept facing the body at all times.

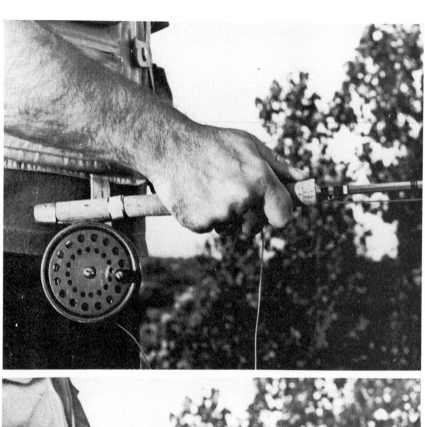

The three grips which are discussed in the text. The above photo portrays the hold least favored by the author. The two other holds are the methods of grip most popular with the majority of anglers.

This style of introduction was the brainchild of Clive Young, the tackle specialist of Harrow in Middlesex, England. His theory was that the person casting the equipment can observe the behavior of the line in the air, correct faults in the aerialization, experiment with the speed of the casting stroke, and see the reaction of the line and, by varying the band of power application, alter the angle of travel of the line and the energy shape it adopts.

Once the pupil has mastered the aerialization of the line to left and right, and is able to keep the line above his head at all times and has even progressed to a stage where the plane of travel can be altered at will, he will have fully realized the spring and lever role that the rod plays; discovered that minimal physical forces are involved and will have found out a great deal about the timing necessary to push the line across the body, and throw it out to the dominant side, then allowing it to straighten, then pulling it back to the subsidiary side. The caster has now reached the stage when another rod length of line should be pulled from the reel, and the same exercise of lateral movement of the line practised.

The caster will realize immediately that with the longer length of line, more power and control, with an element of delay, are required (with the shorter line, less power and a faster casting action were necessary) to allow the longer line to extend before it can be brought back on the same plane in the opposite direction. A line unfurling from below has been moved too soon, while an over late stroke will allow the line to hit the ground. "Cracking" off a fly is the result of a much too early delivery.

It is the forearm and wrist that dominate the casting act, forcing the rod to react to the speed and power they exert. The rod, by an energy mix of flex and recoil, pushes and pulls the line back and forth. The next step is to bring more of the basic casting procedures into the casting lesson. Have the pupil grip the elbow of the casting arm with the secondary hand at a point of the midriff that places the dominant hand at chin level with the rod held at a forty-five degree angle from the body. The same lateral movement of the line is again produced by a much more decisive arm and wrist motion with the rod. This rather restrictive casting drill will create for the pupil an appreciation of the task the rod performs and the caster will learn the most effective method of power application to produce the best results in both a visual and practical manner as the rod is worked and the line is manipulated from side to side.

Once this skill has been acquired, and the limited amount of physical movement and power necessary is fully appreciated by the pupil, and the instinctive rhythm and timing that quickly develops are instilled, another facet of fly casting must be introduced.

The secondary hand is used to pull back, then feed out, a few feet of line while the line is still cast in the lateral direction across the body. To feed and retrieve line, the forefinger of the rod hand that holds the line to the handle relaxes the pressure. The gradual shortening and lenghtening of the aerialized line serves to still further sharpen the caster's appreciation of the elements of synchronization in fly fishing — timing (speed) and power (strength).

As soon as this last exercise can be done competently, it requires only a quarter turn of the body and feet, with the line still continued to be cast along the same course, and we have the cast being executed not from the lateral instructional standpoint but from the front-to-rear practical angling position.

Of course it is not possible to observe the line on the backcast without turning the head, but one has to rely upon the ingrained knowledge of instinctive timing that has been learned — the correct amount of power applied to a specific stretch of line and the space of time which must be allowed in order that it may extend fully to the rear before being brought forward.

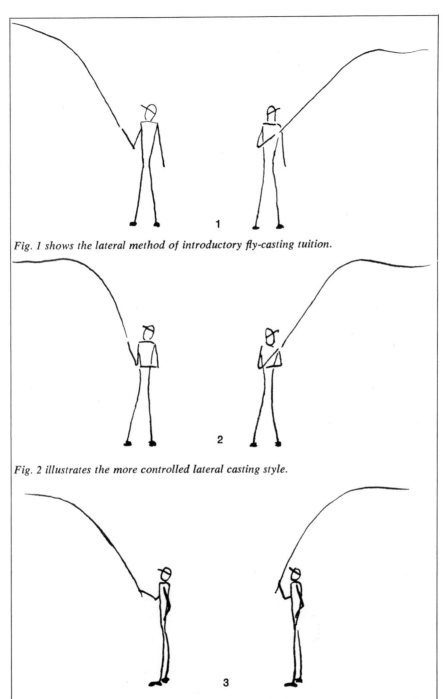

Fig. 1 shows the lateral method of introductory fly-casting tuition.

Fig. 2 illustrates the more controlled lateral casting style.

Fig. 3 depicts the quarter turn necessary to produce the front-to-rear casting procedure.

The first unrestricted rod movements of the lateral method of casting tuition.

The restricted rod movements of the advanced method of the lateral method of instruction.

Continuing to use the directional planes of the lateral casting lesson, where a quarter turn is made by the pupil, the flight of travel becomes the front and rear motion of line movement.

FALSE CASTING

The stages previously explained, once learned, serve dual roles. Not only are they a simple, quickly understood instructional exercise in fly casting, they also represent the action of "false-casting," a fly-fishing procedure used when the line is lengthened and shortened in the air, when a floating fly is being dried off; when stealthy progress is being made along a stream; or when the utmost accuracy of line placement is desired.

A rather innovative method of line control was explained to me by a New Zealand rainbow trout angler, Bill Morris. His method of perfecting his casting was to walk briskly around a field while false casting, changing direction and pace continually. This exercise gave him unbelievable dominance over his equipment. Under certain conditions such as fishing lakes where shoals of surface-feeding fish are cruising fast and fishermen are standing waist deep pumping long, aerialized lines back and forth, while looking for signs of rising fish within casting range, Bill, with his vastly superior line control, is able to cover a fish much faster than most. There are not many fly casters capable of doing a jog trot across a promontory to re-encounter a fast-feeding shoal with a substantial amount of line being held in the air by false casting. Believe me it can be done. It works and I can recommend the method . . . whether all anglers fish at a fast trot in New Zealand, or if the method is Bill Morris' own innovation I do not know, but the degree of line control it creates greatly increases the skill of the angler who practises it!

THE OVERHEAD CAST

The next lesson is the pickup of an extended line from the ground into the backcast, and the forward delivery which places the line back to the original pickup position.

There is scarcely a person receiving casting instruction who has not witnessed the action of an experienced fly caster picking the line from the water, the rod flexing, the line streaming delightfully to the rear, the rod straightening momentarily, then flexing once more as the line is stroked beautifully forward back to the water in a fluid casting motion. This is a clearly etched picture in the mind of the beholder, yet his first attempts at emulating this act are normally disastrous failures, with buggy-whip flailings of rod and line, dreadful see-saw rod manipulations and exaggerated movements, *unless lateral casting has been practised first.*

It is best to stand with the foot of the side opposite to that of the hand that holds the rod leading slightly with the weight of the body evenly distributed over both feet, in a rather boxer-like, balanced stance.

A detailed explanation of the physical application of power within the act of casting, and what movements occur inside the whole motion of casting should help clarify for the newcomer what actually happens when the cast is executed. There is a greater comprehension when the various inter-related actions that take place during the sequence of the cast are separated, and the segments which merge with each other to produce the subtle fluidity of the act are dealt with individually.

For the overhead cast, we start with three times the length of line as the rod is long, with the wool representing the fly attached to the leader, all fully extended to the front.

With the feet and body in the stance previously described, and the rod gripped with the hammer hold and held parallel to the ground, the line anchored to the handle by the forefinger, the wrist is turned down and locked in that position, and the forearm is held on the same plane as the rod, with the upper arm hanging loosely from the shoulder.

The rod is held firmly, but not tightly, and the first part of the lift-off is "forearm lift". Simply by raising the arm from the elbow in an accelerating motion, the rod is tilted upwards. This has the effect of drawing the line towards the caster. On water, with a floating line there is surface resistance and with a sunk line an even greater hold will be exerted by the water, causing the rod to flex and assist the casting action.

It should be noted that there is more weight (tension) involved when lifting the line from water than when picking it up from grass, a paved area, or the floor of a gymnasium, a fact which is never stressed sufficiently. I have witnessed many times the graduates of some winter-casting course completely nonplussed when confronted by water after three months of friction-free lift-offs and floor-bouncing frontal deliveries. To adapt from a solid to a liquid casting situation requires a more powerful lift and a higher forward stroke.

Regardless of the situation, the lift-off is a smooth, accelerating movement. The action is culminated with a firm upward wrist motion, applied when the hand holding the rod reaches chin level.

From just holding the rod handle on the upward forearm lift (at this point of travel at chin height), the grip is tightened and the wrist is used to inject a final pulse of rod movement, which lifts the line into the backcast almost, but not completely, halting the rod at the vertical, where the grip on the handle is relaxed to the previous tension. The hand is now placed at eye level and the rod tip is tilted slightly towards the rear.

The arm-and-wrist casting motion can be practised, believe it or not, by simply holding a pencil. This actually enables the caster to analyze the move carefully without distraction of rod flex and line travel. Wrist locked down . . . forearm lift . . . smooth increase of speed . . . wrist flicked up, and halted at the vertical, producing what is perhaps best described as a crescendo of power contained within an accelerated casting stroke.

The pencil exercise both visually and physically demonstrates the complete overhead casting procedure, and should be used whenever a problem in casting is encountered.

In tournament fly-casting jargon, the wrist is "blocked" after the kicking motion which the wrist applied traveling from the "locked down" starting position through possibly two-thirds of the arc of movement the wrist joint is capable of producing, the "kick" being done at chin level as the arm moved upwards.

Any further backward motion of rod and hand is "drift" in tourney language and, when done, serves only to keep in contact and maintain control of the backward moving line. Drifting will be described more fully when the haul technique of fly casting is explained. The action of the wrist is one of the main ingredients of the cast, and the correct application of the wrist motion is a deciding factor of the efficiency of the execution.

"Drift" is actually the motion of deceleration after the line has been thrown to the front or rear, and is concealed inside the rhythm and synchronization of the timing of the cast. If the accelerating motion contained within the rhythmic casting action can be explained (and understood) as being a crescendo of power, then the rod drift to the rear or on to the follow-through after frontal delivery can justifiably be described as the diminuendo of the casting movement.

Without lateral-casting instruction, there is invariably a tendency to open the wrist motion completely, to the extent that the rod tip almost touches the ground behind the caster and throws the line down to the rear. Should this fault prove a serious problem with a pupil, the butt of the rod should be stuck into the jacket sleeve, or a piece of string tied from the reel seat around the wrist, leaving a space that allows a three-finger drink measure between rod and wrist with the cord. This will stop any see-saw tendencies of the wrist with the rod.

It is rather strange that the majority of fly casters who develop this fault never search for the solution to their casting problem, but appear to live with the situation of losing flies and getting snagged, accepting it as a normal tribulation of fly fishing.

Illustrations Pages 72-73.

The Sequence of the Cast — Starts lower left, with wrist locked down.

Middle left shows the forearm lift completed (the grip is tightened) and the wrist is about to add the final impulse to upward motion. Top left, acceleration completed, the grip is relaxed and the rod has drifted back in readiness for the frontal delivery.

Top right shows the drawing forward of the line and the start of the downward forearm motion. Middle right shows a halting of arm movement (the grip is tightened). The wrist action is about to be introduced into the cast. At bottom right, the wrist has been turned down, adding a final thrust of power to the forward delivery.

Scanning the rod positions in the six photographs, from lower left to bottom right, will assist the reader in his appreciation of the arm, wrist, hand, and rod movements during the casting action.

3

2

1

Psychologically, if the caster attempts to throw the line up above his head, the correct result will be achieved. The line will be thrown back high, (the laws of gravity dictate that it must fall eventually as it unfurls to the rear) and, at the point of complete rearward extension, while momentarily hanging parallel in the air, will be drawn forward into the frontal delivery.

The physical action contained in the forward part of the cast in order to lay the line on the water is done by first applying a gentle forward pulling arm motion that merges into a downward accelerating chopping action of the forearm from chin to chest. The grip on the handle of the rod tightens and the wrist is turned smoothly down (from the blocked position). This gently, yet positively, draws and then drives the line forward, after which there is an element of followthrough in some respects similar to the drift on the backcast in the arm movement which returns arm, hand, and rod to approximately the same position as at the start of the lift-off.

Some casters tend to reach forward on the frontal delivery, with a sword-like thrusting action of the rod. When this is done, it is basically the caster performing a task that the rod should be executing. This is quite a minor fault when compared to the flailing rod motions that are often seen when an angler, to achieve the end results necessary to cast and extend the line, uses the complete arm and a lot of body movement. Thankfully, this fault, due to the transaction from cane to glass, is not encountered as frequently as it was. Cane, because of its weight distribution was almost self-casting, while glass had to be "worked", and presented a problem that some anglers could not overcome.

In 1950, Captain Tommy Edwards was a leading casting authority and angling instructor, and he described the forward delivery as being similar to driving a nail at waist level into a wooden fence with a hammer. The many thousands of fishermen he taught so successfully endorse his teaching. The dozens of tourney casters he coached and who are now instructors and casting experts are a splendid testimonial to his work. It was he who explained to a group of us during a lull in the events of a British Casting Championship, about the hold on the rod handle. Tommy told us that the grip was tightened and relaxed within the cast to achieve maximum results. Excessive strength used to grip the rod caused vibrational restriction on line flow, affected aerialized line behavior, and greatly influenced overall casting performance.

To recap, here is a concise verbal description of the overhead cast, physical motion, rod action, and line movement, from lift-off to the setting down of the line:

With rod and forearm parallel to the ground, and the line extended to the front, with the wrist locked down, start forearm lift; aim to produce a smooth accelerating motion; the rod flexes; when the hand is at chin level, the grasp on the handle is tightened and the wrist adds a final surge of power to speed the line to the rear in a high backward direction. The grip on the rod is relaxed. As this happens the rod compresses further to overcome the weight and speed of the line. Then, on recoil, throws the line to the rear. There is a momentary pause to allow the line to extend, which is the point where rod drift occurs, the caster tipping the top of the rod to the rear, and following the course of the line as it unfurls to the utmost limits of the backward extension and, at that instant, the forearm pushes to the front, speeding up as it starts to chop down at chest height. Pulling the line forward at an increased speed, the flexed rod once more reacts to the compressional load. The hand again grasps the handle firmly and the wrist is turned down. The line is pulled to the front as the rod recovers from the compressed state of flex. The arm motion decelerates and arrives at the original starting position, and the line extends to the front and falls.

The action of the overhead cast can be done holding the rod at any angle and executed on any plane, from a delivery made from above the head, to a level of travel just above the surface of the water. When actual angling conditions are encountered, if this has been practised, the ability to control the equipment to this degree of expertise will prove enormously valuable to the fly caster, for example, when a line must be thrown beneath the overhanging branches of trees, or when the wind is troublesome and the line and fly are to be kept away from the face and eyes of the angler, or, if two people are fishing from a boat.

Once this degree of control has been learnt, the role of fly-fishing tackle can be broadened and, as the use of the equipment is further expanded, a greater realization of the fantastic versatility of the tackle at the disposal of the fly fisherman can be appreciated to the full.

The energy of the cast is created by the physical effort of the caster; converted into kinetic impulse by the rod motion and flexural actions; and finally transferred to the line movement and travel pattern. This is perhaps best and most simply explained by recalling the childhood act of tying a skipping rope to a tree and shaking the loose end up and down to make a snake ripple travel along the line. The wave-like undulation passed along the rope by snapping the arm down is an impulse of kinetic energy. This is the motivational energy used to cast a fly line.

THE ROLL CAST

A cast made on the water utilizes the same kinetic impulse as was created by the child with the skipping rope. It is called, very aptly, the roll cast, because the line rolls out when put into motion. There are various methods of making a roll cast with complex rod-travel patterns and line manipulations. One of the most famous is the Double Spey Cast. To keep everything in perspective, let me quote Tommy Edwards: "There are only two methods of casting a fly, one done with the line in the air (the aerialized cast) and the other made with the line on the water (the roll)." Any variation of these basics does not alter whatsoever the grouping to which they belong, and anyone attempting to complicate the matter with new terminology was informed of the basic principles in no uncertain manner by "the Cap'n." *It is not difficult, so keep it simple!*

The roll is a very simple cast to perform, and a rod paired with a floating line, used on a still area of water is the best place to learn it. First, the leader at this stage still with the wool representing the bulk of the fly attached to it and a yard or so of the line, is deposited on the water where it will stay gripped in the surface film. A few more feet of line is then stripped from the reel, and with the rod tilted down, by gently moving the tip back and forth, more line is stroked on to the water. On moving water, the current would take hold of the line and it would drift away, thus making the job of feeding out more line less difficult. When on still areas of water it is best to move a foot or so along the bank after each deposit, accumulating the line to the side that the angler casts from — to the right for a right-handed angler and to the left if that is the dominant side of the caster.

Practise with about four rod lengths of line. If a double-tapered line is being used, the pupil may start the lesson. If a weight-forward line is used, care must be taken to ensure that only the heavy portion of the line is being cast and the fine running line is contained within the rod guides, as the small diameter line cannot accept sufficient energy (absorb enough kinetic impulse) to push the heavier section ahead of it.

With the line so located, the rod is raised in an unhurried manner to the vertical and tilted back to the drift position with the hand held at eye level and positioned about twelve inches from the head. The line will follow the tip of the rod, and a loop of line will hang from the tip to the rear of the caster, then down to the water, where it will lie on the surface at right angles to the angler.

The casting motion for executing the roll cast is similar in all respects to that used for the frontal delivery of the overhead cast. There is a forward pushing motion of the forearm, followed by a pronounced, accelerating forearm hammer stroke which is finalized with a downward turn of the wrist. The power stroke of the rod starts at the vertical, finishes at waist level, and contains the same crescendo of strength and momentum. The rod moves from an upright position down to a parallel plane, with a follow-through movement that brings the rod to a halt about a foot above the water.

The first cast will roll the line out. The angler will immediately appreciate the fundamentals of the roll cast — the hammer stroke made with the rod driving a bolt of energy down the line and the surge of power traveling along the line producing the "rolling" action which gradually loses strength as each portion it passes along serves to lift and turn the section ahead. The tapered line is completely allied to the decreasing energy traveling along its length. It is the directional motion of the rod that dictates the course of line. The line will always attempt to extend in the direction finally imposed by the path of the rod. This is a fact of the mechanics of the cast that remains as true today as the first recorded side-arm throw with a fly spoken of by Aelian.

On still water the line will remain in the position it was deposited. The rod should again be slowly lifted to the vertical, the bag of line once more allowed to fall to the rear of the caster, and another pulse of motion imparted to the line by the downward casting stroke. Should the line not completely unfurl, two or three feet of it should be stripped back and the roll cast repeated until it is performed correctly.

On moving water, after the cast has been completed, the line is carried downstream by the current, finishing below the angler. Providing the strength of the stream is not too severe and the fisherman can create a bag of line to the rear, the roll cast may be executed quite efficiently, without any consideration being given to the angle of the line, as the line will follow the course dictated by the energizing motion of the casting stroke produced by the rod. The placement of the line on still water with the line deposited to the side of the caster is a factual exercise in the angling situation that will be encountered on a river, where the current sweeps the line downstream as the cast is fished out. The roll cast is used to place the line across the water where the fly is fished as the current swings it towards the near bank.

When the angler can roll out the line with a decisive rod movement, can repeatedly turn the length over positively, and has complete control of directional placement, he should experiment with the roll cast using longer and shorter lengths of line.

The roll cast is used when obstructions such as trees, high banks, or lack of space make it impossible to use the aerialized cast. It has tremendous angling value to the fly fisherman. It can be executed from either side of the body (although done best from the dominant side with the line located in that area) and a cross-body movement with the rod from the distal side when the line is in that position will produce a roll cast if the principles of the cast are observed.

In Britain not too many years ago distance roll casting competitions were held for salmon fishermen, who used production rods that measured up to eighteen feet in length and were cast double handed. These magnificent rods were made from either greenheart or double-built split cane. They

Illustrations Pages 78-79.
The roll cast, starting from the lower left, upwards, across, and down to the bottom right. The method is demonstrated using a fast sinking, double-tapered line, which necessitates that the line be pulled towards the caster, then swung to the rear, after which the bag of line behind the angler is driven forward.

78

4

5

6

were matched with heavy silk lines of both double and single-taper profiles and casts measuring over forty-five yards were recorded. The competitions normally took place on some river pool that had a casting platform built out into the current, with the casting being done downstream. A roll cast of over forty yards is a truly awesome feat. The next time you are fishing pace this distance out and pause a moment in respect of those halcyon days when the big rod reigned supreme.

THE SPEY CAST

The technique used to execute the Spey Cast is of use to the trout fly fisherman as well as the salmon angler. It is employed when the line hangs downstream of the angler and must be extended across the current.

The rod is lifted to the vertical. The pull of the current should lift the line in contact with the water, to the surface. If the line is deeply sunk, a downstream roll cast must be made to lift line, leader, and fly to the top. With a jerking wrist action, and a decisive tilt of the rod tip, the line is thrown upstream in a loose bag that deposits the skidded fly on the water just above the position where the angler is stationed, with the main loop of the line falling higher upstream. As the fly skips across the front of the angler, and the line is still traveling upstream, swing the rod to the side, then to the rear, and then to an upright position with a circular motion and with the rod held at a vertical angle. This action, executed without undue violence, exerts sufficient momentum to the line to fling a moving loop to the rear, which is immediately driven forward in the normal roll-cast manner to extend the line across the current.

Spey casting is a form of roll cast which is very punishing to the rod, because of the twisting nature of the rod movement produced to execute the cast. The right rods were the spliced greenheart rods, consisting of three seven-foot sections, made on Speyside. The most famous make was the 'Grant's Vibration", a fabulous, slow action, spliced rod. They were made from the densest sections of the wood, and were "hand riven" (split by hand), rounded, heat straightened, and tapered, then carefully matched with sections of equally dense grain. For many years I used an old Hardy "High Regan" that caught many fish. It was given to me by Angus Robertson who shared duties with Tom Young, now only illustrious names on the list of boatmen associated with the North Wark beat on the River Tweed. The "High Regan" was a three-section, seventeen-foot powerhouse, that provided my father and myself with eight late season salmon averaging over twenty pounds from Number Two Beat at Coldstream. I have never beaten this record.

One should be getting an appreciation of the capabilities that lie dormant in the equipment used by the fly fisherman. For example, a considerable amount of line can be cast out by an adaptation of the principles of the roll. In a "one cast only" spot, completely surrounded by trees, by depositing the required amount of line on to the water, or, half in the water and the rest laid on the ground at the feet of the angler, a bag of line is placed by hand to the rear, and the roll cast is made with a firm driving stroke.

THE STEEPLE CAST

The Steeple Cast is a method of lift into the overhead cast that is a novel style of lift-off. It aerializes a similar deposit of line lying at the feet of the fly fisherman producing a high soaring backcast by the application of the maximum forearm-lifting motion possible before an upward thrust of the wrist. But again let me stress it is but a variation of the basic casting motion contained within the rudimentary mechanics of the backcast.

DELIVERY ZONES

Now that the student fly caster has a greater awareness of the transmission of power from the rod to the line that was first discovered during the lateral exercise with the aerialized line; then applied to the fore and aft direction of travel with the overhead method; further clarified by the visual appreciation of the energies producing the roll; there should be, at this stage, a better grasp of the mechanics of the cast. An understanding of the principles involved invariably builds confidence, and results in progress in the art of casting a fly.

The next step is to increase the caster's versatility by broadening his ability to use the tackle, both in aerialized and roll-cast methods of fly casting. A line will always attempt to follow the direction of movement imparted by the rod, and the form the line adopts as it travels in the air or upon the water (the shape it assumes while unfurling) is controlled by the type of impulse generated by the caster, and results from the application of energy that is transmitted by the casting action, which ultimately governs the efficiency of the cast.

A directional change of the roll cast on water is achieved by ignoring the placement of the line and is done simply by driving the bag of line behind the rod to the area where the line is required. The roll cast can be executed with the rod held at any angle, from a vertical position where the hammer stroke is used to extend the line, to a slicing forehand drive motion made on a plane parallel to the water. The only constant factor is the bag of loose line behind the rod. It has to accept a surge of kinetic energy of sufficient force to travel down the line in order to extend it in the direction the rod is pointing. In all casting situations the physical movement consists of a forearm motion culminating with a turning of the wrist which, in turn, dominates rod travel, dictates rod movement, and creates the energy impulse transmitted to the line.

From my own experience of giving casting instruction, I have found the roll cast to be the ideal method of casting to instruct the student on yet another aspect of the mechanics of casting, that is, the various zones of power application that control line behavior (and naturally angling procedures) contained within the frontal delivery of the cast.

Using the roll cast as the medium to explain the zones of power available for the frontal delivery of the cast, the angler is instructed to extend the line in a positive manner. This will result in a long, strong, chopping stroke, a low delivery made at waist level, and a decisive roll of energy unfurling the line to maximum extension on the water, with the final dying bolt of kinetic energy flipping the wool tied to the end of the leader out of the water and plinking it back to the surface in the classically executed roll cast.

With the next roll cast, the pupil is instructed to apply the maximum power and wrist turn at chest level, compressing the area of arm travel into a shorter casting stroke. The result will be a much higher peak of line roll as it unfurls, making the section of line that was held on the surface nearest the rod rise up from the water when the more concentrated power impulse passes through it. The fly will be lifted high from the water before dropping back to the surface, with the leader loosely tumbled about, which is a far from satisfactory angling cast. However, the object of the exercise is to illustrate clearly the power zones the angler can produce from the tackle by the casting method.

Finally, the caster is instructed to shorten still further the degree of arm movement, concentrate still more the arc of the power stroke, and execute the crescendo of speed and strength within a smaller band of accelerated motion throwing the roll cast out at chin level. This forward stroke if done correctly will lift the complete line from the water and, when sufficient power has been generated from the casting motion, there will be an instant when the line is lifted clear of the surface. During this split second of suspension, there is enough time to enable the angler to pull the line from the aerialized position created from the high frontal delivery of the roll cast, into the backcast. This style of cast has the effect of creating an aerialized forward delivery situation, developed from the energy reaction of the line.

Such a type of line pickup from the water, using the high delivery to aerialize the line, is a casting technique used by dry-fly fishermen to pluck a fly from the surface that ordinarily would be drawn beneath the water if the normal lift-off method of casting were employed.

If the roll cast is observed from the side where the surge of power traveling down the line can be clearly seen, the energies of the angler's cast are more readily understood.

82

One summer some years ago I worked on the Scottish Tourist Board Angling Course at Tweed Valley with Peter Anderson, a splendid fisherman and a caster who has dominated the British casting scene for many years. To demonstrate the energies of the roll cast and the techniques involved to produce the various delivery planes, we tied a leader to the resilient tree branch bordering the lawns of the Tweed Valley Hotel. The preparatory instructional work had been done on grass before taking our pupils down to fish on the banks of the Tweed.

We used a twenty-yard length of line through the rod and grouped the anglers to the side. By applying various styles of delivery, different power planes, and dissimilar rod motions, we demonstrated the shapes of the energy forms as the line accepted them in this way. As these impulses passed along the line, we showed what methods of delivery produced the most satisfactory results. The lesson always proved to be most educational and instructive. It helped, better than any other way, to communicate to the pupils the energy produced from the cast.

Assuming a pupil has learned the art of casting in the progression I have outlined, with the lateral and overhead casts practised under "dry" conditions, and the roll done on the first encounter with the liquid element, the first experience of the lift-off into the aerialized overhead cast from water can be attempted.

If the arm-lifting and wrist-kicking motions were clearly incorporated into the casting movement, the student will appreciate more fully the acceleration of the lift, and the crescendo of power that has been constantly referred to in our previous discussions of basic technique and rudimentary casting mechanics. On water, the lift of the forearm glides the line towards the angler at a steadily increasing speed and, at the point approaching the upward turn of the wrist, the line slides from the surface on an upward plane of aerialized motion. This should be a soundless, sliding, smooth, gliding, accelerating movement. Should any sound of ripping water be produced by the line being torn from the surface, the crescendo of speed and power is being applied by the caster with a motion which is too fast, too short, or is done in a burst of speed that executes the cast jerkily.

A wrinkle of tourney knowledge that will prove of use to the fly fisherman when a change of direction is necessary (in accuracy events or on the river): the position of the line is ignored, the rod is pointed at the spot towards which the line will be cast (a target or a rising fish), and then the lift-off is made. A change of direction executed in this manner allows the line to swing to the rear while adopting the new angle of travel. The forward stroke of the new direction of delivery is fully accepted by the line without any motional energy being wasted changing course through the air. This results in superior line control, greater accuracy, and better presentation.

In the aerialized cast, the three zones of frontal delivery are a very necessary facet of fly fishing, for without the ability to produce the forward cast on various planes and the presentation of the line from different levels, the skills of fly fishing are limited.

We know direction comes from pointing the rod at the position to which the line will extend and, in the case of the overhead aerialized line, as long as the rod passes back and forth through the plane of sight, the line will unfurl and extend in that direction as though the line were extruded from the tip of the rod.

Zone One area of the frontal presentation of the overhead cast is produced when the forward stroke is delivered to the front in a casting motion performed from ear to chin. This produces an extension of the aerialized line above the water and deposits the fly, leader, and line on to the water at the same time. It gives a most gentle presentation and, should the angler wish to deposit loose line, there is enough time after the forward delivery stroke to gently wave the rod from side to side and create a loose snaking extension of the line when it falls to the water. This high release point can be used when there is a following wind, as it will be found that the line extends with a minimum of casting effort (although of course more power must be used to push the line into the wind on the backcast). When using a dry fly, it helps to aim at a point one or two feet above the place where the fly is to be dropped. If the high delivery is used, it will produce a natural, feather-light presentation.

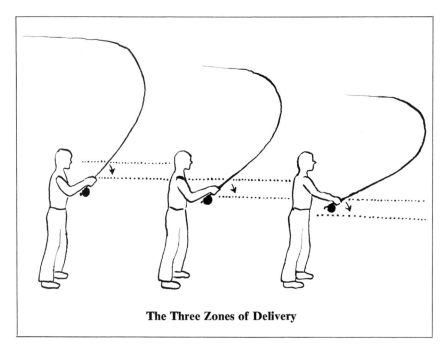

The Three Zones of Delivery

Zone Two of the forward delivery is contained in a casting stroke made from chin to chest. It is the normal frontal delivery explained in our earlier description of the overhead technique of casting. This method of line presentation is generally used more often than any other in the casting of a fly. Aim for a point six to twelve inches above the water where the fly is intended to fall (which results from practice). This causes the least disturbance of the water when the line is put down on the surface.

The lowest delivery of the line is also the most positive. It is produced from Zone Three of power application and, for this stroke, the energy comes from a point opposite the rib cage to below the waist. This delivery is used when a fly must be placed positively in a spot where delicate presentation is unnecessary or less essential than placement, for example, into a pocket of water behind a boulder, or to a riffle below a half-submerged log. However, the cast is tremendously efficient when a line must be driven into the wind. In a wind, the combination of a tight loop and a low delivery will knife the line to an extension in wind that would make angling impossible, without a command of the three zones of delivery.

These three forward delivery planes, once mastered, broaden immensely the repertoire of presentation, and vastly increase the angling versatility of the fisherman. When lighter power outfits are used, the three casting zones are made with strokes that can be compared to the delicate movements of the artist's brush on a canvas. With middle-power equipment, the delivery is rather similar to making positive chalk marks on a wall, and when the strongest tackle is being employed, the areas of forward release are done as one would make a deep mark on a timber surface with a six-inch nail. However, all the strokes are executed at the same positions — the first from eye to chin, the second from neck to chest, and the third from ribcage to hip.

The three zones of frontal delivery and the areas of power application must be learnt and practised until they are instinctive, for they contain the essential elements and skills necessary to fully master the art of fly fishing. At this time I consider it pertinent to add that, regardless of the plane of the forward delivery, the travel of the line on the backcast remains more or less constant — thrown as high as possible, the power applied as smoothly as can be done, and brought forward at the instant of full extension. Always bear in mind that without a good backcast, a satisfactory frontal delivery cannot be achieved.

A line follows the course dictated by the rod which is, in turn, moved by the angler. Any slicing effect contained within the course of rod movement robs the line of speed, as energy is lost changing the angle of travel on the unfurling journey back and forth. The rod, for maximum performance and power transference, should move as though contained within an imaginary slot — from front to rear.

The Basis of Line Shape

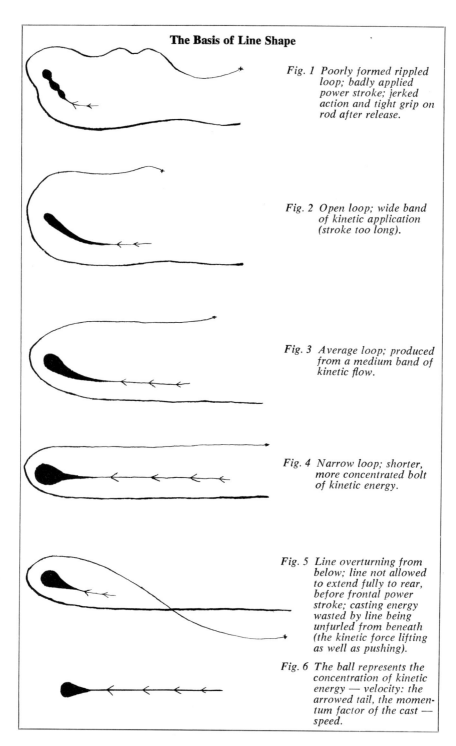

Fig. 1 Poorly formed rippled loop; badly applied power stroke; jerked action and tight grip on rod after release.

Fig. 2 Open loop; wide band of kinetic application (stroke too long).

Fig. 3 Average loop; produced from a medium band of kinetic flow.

Fig. 4 Narrow loop; shorter, more concentrated bolt of kinetic energy.

Fig. 5 Line overturning from below; line not allowed to extend fully to rear, before frontal power stroke; casting energy wasted by line being unfurled from beneath (the kinetic force lifting as well as pushing).

Fig. 6 The ball represents the concentration of kinetic energy — velocity: the arrowed tail, the momentum factor of the cast — speed.

A narrow loop or a wide loop; a smooth curve or a waved irregular form, when observed in an aerialized line, shows the shape of the energy impulse imparted to it by the casting movement. I have attended lectures by anglers who talk of *air resistance* affecting the performance of the line. Perhaps for the average angler this explanation is sufficient when discussing loop shapes. The more concentrated the surge of power, the tighter will be the loop, and the faster and farther it will travel. The broader the stroke, the wider will be the band of energy, the more open the loop, the more slowly will it move and the less distance it will carry. Air *friction* must enter into the matter of line motion, as does gravitational pull. However, the truth is that line performance is controlled by the power application and the method and tackle used to produce it.

A line cannot travel like a javelin through the air. After it extends it must fall on a slightly angled descending course from the momentum of the kinetic impulse traveling through it (the loop at its center contains the surge of energy, the lower section is pulled along and the upper portion pushed ahead). Some of the more expert casting instructors can diagnose faults in timing, grip, and casting stroke by simply watching the progress of a line through the air.

The extended line after the final delivery never lies. Should it bounce back after delivery, too much power was applied. When it collapses, insufficient energy was used or a bad casting stroke robbed the line of speed. Snakes and bends are usually caused from gripping the handle of the rod too tightly or from bad timing, and when there is a pronounced curve in the line to the left or right, the rod has been moved back and forth on curved planes of travel.

While the correct casting methods have been outlined in the preceding pages, and are the standard methods of instruction, the required end result (precise and delicate placement, paired with dominant and efficient line control), may be achieved by the use of styles completely alien to those I have described. I once taught a dentist who had a grip so strong that he cast with his fingers more easily and efficiently than he could by arm and wrist motion, manipulating the rod with thumb and the first two fingers.

In all things, and particularly angling, dogma must be avoided at all costs. The methods for the casting of a fly, outlined here, have proved satisfactory up to this point in time, yet some development must lie ahead for this is the way progress unfolds. From the side arm throw spoken of by Aelian, the rod-waving technique of Cotton, the sweeping (and stately) strokes of Halford, to the superior casting action provided by the tackle of the present day, something different still lies ahead.

SHOOTING EXTRA LINE

Once the delivery zones of the frontal delivery of the aerialized cast have been thoroughly mastered, the technique of line shooting can be

Shooting Line — Here the loose line is drawn through the rod guides, after the main casting length. It is imperative, when attempting to shoot extra line, that the forward delivery has been fully executed and the line driven to the front, before the shooting line is released. It is the motion of the casting length which provides the energy to pull the shooting line behind it.

learned. Up to this point, during the progression of casting instruction, the line has been anchored firmly to the fly rod handle by the forefinger (except for the one short period when line was fed and retrieved through the rod guides, as the speed and power adjustments were made to the casting action during the final stages of the lateral casting lesson). The line, when locked tightly to the rod, accepts the full levering motion of the casting stroke and receives the whole movement of decompressional thrust from the rod as it springs back from the flexed position.

When the angler is able to cast competently with the tackle held in this manner, the next stage is to involve the secondary hand in the casting motion. In actual fishing practice, when the fly is being fished and the line retrieved, finger control of the line by the hand gripping the rod is an essential contributing element of emphatic contact with the feathered offering through the rod to the angler. When casting out, however, it is not done.

The preparation to shoot line is done by extending to the front of the angler nearly the maximum amount of line that he is able to cast, and then stripping from the reel a length of line measuring perhaps eight or ten feet which is deposited on the ground to the opposite side of the body to that which holds the rod.

When this is done, all is ready for the lift-off. With the dominant hand positioned for the forearm lift, the secondary hand reaches forward and firmly grips the line as high up on the rod as is comfortable. As the lift begins and the casting arm is raised, the secondary hand draws back the line at a steadily increasing speed. When the wrist imparts the final impact of rearward motion to the rod, the hand pulling the line is halted at a position near the hip, having added an extra surge of speed to the casting movement. This two-handed accelerating action (one hand traveling upwards from the starting point, the other moving back to the body) has the dual effect of adding greater speed to the line on lift-off and producing more flexibility, and therefore greater recoil power from the rod.

On the frontal delivery, the line should be driven forward with the rod in the normal manner and, as the line starts to unfurl to the front (the caster should watch for this to occur, as it helps the synchronization of the action), the secondary hand releases the line it holds.

If the cast is done as described, the forward delivery of the line should have sufficient momentum to draw after it the line that was stripped from the reel and dropped on the ground. There is only one fault to watch out for, and that is the tendency of the pupil to release the line too early.

The sequence of the successful line shoot is achieved by driving the line forward and then releasing the reserve amount which "shoots" through the guides, from which originates the name of the cast. The extra line is pulled through the guides after the unfurling aerialized line which is moving towards a point of frontal extension that has been lengthened by the amount of line drawn behind it, unhindered by any restraint from the rod.

A similar shooting of line can be done for the roll cast: the bag of line is driven forward and then the additional line is fed into the cast.

The shooting of extra line enables the fly fisherman to cast farther with less effort and, when combined with a high delivery of an aerialized cast, provides a gentler, more gliding presentation of line, leader, and fly on to the surface of the water, even though basically the technique is used to obtain extra distance.

Knowledge and expertise gained from the tournament game is continually being applied to aspects of practical fly-fishing technique. Great contributions were made to the sport by pioneers like Marvin Hedge of the U.S.A., and the three generations of the Hardy family, Edgar May and Tommy Edwards of Britain, and were brought closer to the present-day by North American and World Champions such as Johnny Dieckmann and Jon E. Tarantino (both of whom died tragically young, Johnny in a plane crash and J.E.T. in an armed robbery at his store). All of them could fish as well as they performed with equipment on the casting platform, which is a point not fully realized by the vast majority of fly fishermen. In the beginning they influenced the design of tackle, later guiding manufacturers, and finally designed the prototypes of fly-rod ranges that are currently in production.

Tournament technique, when related to angling method, broadens the horizons of the sport, and undoubtedly increases the versatility of the fly fisherman. From the ranks of the American Casting Association, the name of Myron Gregory of California immediately comes to mind as one of the finest instructors, and undoubtedly one of the greatest casting technicians ever. He has applied tournament method and design of tackle to practical angling for both saltwater and river fishing with tremendous success and great hopes are placed on the current world champion, Steve Rajeff. Then there is Jim Green of Washington, a truly fantastic fly accuracy caster, who is in charge of development and rod design for an international tackle manufacturer. Britain has her counterparts, such as Jack Martin, a fine all-around caster who is employed by a major fly-line production company, and Peter Anderson, possibly the best caster Britain has ever produced who is retained by a leading tackle company.

It is unnecessary to continue as the list is substantial. However, it is sufficient to say that all facets of the tackle industry have some degree of contact, from information to involvement, with developments that occur on the tournament circuit.

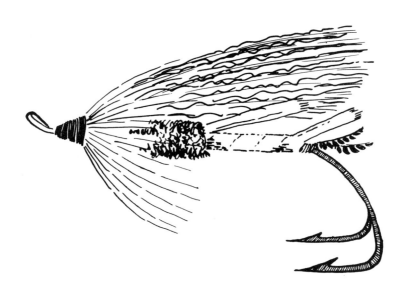

CHAPTER 5

The Powers behind the Cast

For the student who finds the integral energies of the cast a subject of interest, further comment is necessary on the mechanical aspects, motional dynamics, and kinetic forces developed from the equipment of the fly caster.

The knowledge that has been accumulated regarding the various energies connected with casting has come from people involved with tournament casting. The facts that have been learned apply to all facets of the angling cast. It is mainly from the experience gained from the distance bait events and the fly-distance competitions, that enlightenment has come. Tournament casting is to angling equipment what car racing is to the vehicle used by the everyday motorist — a testing ground.

Casting energy is generated by the physical action of the angler: within the casting motion, the rod by flexational recoil adds the predominant thrust of power to the fly line (the casting weight); which unfurls (rolls) to extension (turnover), by the kinetic impulse of travel.

The energies which are applied by the angler's cast and produced from the tackle employed are quite unique, for whatever is being cast must reverse its mass with every casting stroke. Whether the weight is a compact spinning lure, terminal tackle consisting of float, lead shot, and a baited hook, a solid, streamlined surf weight, or a pliable fly line — all must turn around completely immediately after the point of maximum speed on delivery i reached. The mass is drawn towards the directional plane on an acceleration course, moving on a line of progress to which its bulk is opposed as the application of power is applied. When the new directional motion is dictated (by the rod) and accepted by the weight (the line), it turns around within the movement of travel (turnover).

The field of kinetic force is a subject that Don Neish (in his day a first-rate British caster, and a pupil of Tommy Edwards), and myself have often discussed in Don's angling store in Edmonton, London. When the kinetics of the line performance are analyzed, the line throughout the period of acceleration accepts movement as a whole, and relative to its sectional mass (weight distribution). However, once a constant speed is attained, the method of propulsion requires that a reversal of mass must occur. The function of the rod when examined becomes still more apparent, and the duties of lever and spring are quite obvious. Consider, for example, the short distance in which the rod actually operates to propel the line back and forth on a level course, a plane of travel at the tip which at maximum is not much more than half the length of the rod when the fly fisherman is viewed standing at the apex of an inverted triangle defined by the area of rod movement. It is the peak of acceleration which causes the point of turnover (the moment speed is constant, the reversal of mass begins). It is the rod which imparts the final thrust of kinetic energy, having up to this instant been kept in a state of compression and, on recoil, transfers a final pulse of speed that is seen traveling along the unfurling aerialized line similar to the energy force moving through the line on the water when the roll cast was performed.

There may now be an appreciation of why a tapered line performs so much better than one of level construction. Speed and weight combine to produce velocity, which to fly casting is a combination of the distance attainable and the degree of control available. A heavier portion of line accepts more energy than a lighter section and, as the kinetic impulse is quickly dissipated by motion, the shape of the line must be that of a wedge to relate to the laws of motional behavior, the energies of the method of propulsion, and the means by which it is applied. The tapered line is a weight, and the rod is a casting tool, and in their roles as pieces of angling equipment, although of great value and the source of tremendous pleasure and aesthetic enjoyment, the saying, "casting comes before catching" puts all in perspective.

A rod can be said to consist of three functional areas. The uppermost portion is the sensitive link between the angler, the line, and the fly, transmitted from the tip to the hand through the rod. The middle area is the source of power from where originates the flex thrust and drive that is passed to the line by the recoil of the rod from compression. The section above the handle is the stiffest area of the rod and controls the speed that the angler can apply to the cast.

Some rods (the basic casting actions) have the three zones of function — link, spring, and lever — evenly spaced. The top third is the sensitive link, the middle third the source of power, and the bottom third a lever. A fast action, in a conventional rod, may have much less of the link element in the tip, but more of the power area, and a slightly longer, stiffer area for the lever butt, while a rod that has a slow action will have little rigidity in the bottom section, and the middle area will merge into the highest portion. Knowing that the drive of casting power has its source from the middle part of the rod length, there are repeated trends by manufacturers to produce "staggered" rod sections (a short butt section and a much longer top section). This method of rod making provides a joint-free area of rod where the recoil flex occurs, creating an uninterrupted power flow. However, the fly fisherman has never accepted the principle of uneven rod sections mainly because of the danger of breakage during transportation and, I suspect, possibly a slight subconscious aesthetic abhorrence towards rods with unequal sectional lengths.

A truly progressive-actioned rod produced from compounded tapers and controlled wall thicknesses from tubular construction, may have the spring and link functions located high in the upper half of the rod, with the lower section performing the role of a lever. When additional stress is placed on it by casting, or applied when playing a fish, the flex is progressively absorbed by the lower area. Such rods are not easy to cast and lack sensitivity. This type of rod does, however, have great overhead-casting capability, and a quite amazing range of performance, but it does not feel good in the hand and has not really had the acceptance it deserves.

The energies required for the roll cast are better applied with a long, slow-actioned rod, as this cast requires a broad injection of motion to be transferred to the line in order that the line may turn over efficiently. The aerialized cast can be thrown farther by a speedy, more condensed stroke and a faster power impulse.

The elements of mechanics, dynamics, and kinetics are similar and define motional forces, yet for a better understanding of the cast, if the *physical actions* of the cast are contained in the *mechanics;* and *dynamics* are used to embrace *rod motion;* and *kinetics* are applied to *line movement,* there will be a better comprehension of the energies of casting by the pupil.

The speed of the recovery of a rod from a state of flex is one of the deciding factors of casting performance. The manner in which the recoil occurs — the speed and smoothness — controls the form of the final energy impulse which is injected into the momentum of the cast and transferred to the motion of the line. We deal here solely with the movement of the rod.

A slow transfer of power imparts a broader band of kinetic force (the wide unfurling loop), while a faster action produces a more concentrated bolt of energy (a tight unrolling loop of line). The narrow and open loops formed by the unfurling line can be thrown with a rod of any action if the angler is armed with the knowledge that the shape the line adopts as it moves through the air is determined by the method and angle of rod travel used for the application of the power stroke. A long, angled stroke produces a wide loop, a short flat stroke a narrow loop. It is, however, a fact that a tighter loop is thrown more easily with the stiffer-actioned rod, the reason being based on the more readily achieved, faster, (and therefore more concentrated) power impulse transferred to the line.

Every material used for the construction of a rod or line reacts in a slightly different manner and just as every musical instrument can be differentiated by tone, so rods of bamboo, glass fiber, and exotic filaments, bonded with phenolic and epoxy resins, and other thermoplastics produce different flex reactions: and lines of silk, nylon, and dacron encased within various polyvinyl coatings, all accept motion differently. The absorbtion of kinetic movement, together with the progress of the wave of energy through them, is quite dissimilar.

A sinking line, because it has a smaller diameter than a floating line of a similar weight assessment is much faster through the air and, for most anglers, the sinker can not be laid upon the water as gently as the floater because of the additional speed the sinking line generates. The mechanics of the casting action are dictated from the quick acceptance of kinetic motion by the thin, heavy line. A faster casting action is required to control the aerialized length, as it has already been established that speed increases the weight factor. The slimmer, heavier, and more pliable a line is the faster will be its progress through the air, as is proved with high-density sinking lines. With the bulky, floating lines, passage through the air is decidedly slower.

Rod speed, together with flex action, are two of the governing factors of the cast (allied of course with the skill of the angler producing) and the marriage of rod length to power assessment has now arrived at a stage of extremely satisfactory performance. Of course there are still specific types of angling where, for example, an eight-foot six-inch line Class Four rod can be very advantageous in a particular fishing technique, and a stiff, five-foot six-inch rod of line Class Six will be the choice of some angling experts. The charts in the preceding pages of this book are a true analysis of the proven requirements for rod length and power rating correlated to line weight and can be applied to any fly-fishing situation anywhere in the world. At this point it would perhaps be opportune to add that details concerning the two-handed casting of ten to fourteen-foot rods, synonomous with European salmon fishing, are contained in a section devoted to this style of two-handed casting.

A stiff rod will cast farther than a rod with a softer action within the same power range, although a stiffer rod is more critical to an error in the timing of a cast. In actual fishing practice, the fast stiff rod is quicker to tighten on to the strike, to hook a fish, but can result in a broken leader point whereas a slow soft rod will cushion a fine tippet from breakage. These elements of rod motion correspond to what has been mentioned at an earlier stage of rapier-like, fast action, dry-fly rods and slow, willow-like, soft action wet-fly rods from another era.

To cast a fly efficiently basically requires that only enough physical strength be applied to decisively control the movement of the rod and dominate the motion of the line which is moving upon a plane of flight within the casting rhythm that contains the subtle timing and synchronization of power application. Physical energy, allied to the mechanics of the cast applied to balanced equipment working in harmony and produced from the dynamics of rod movement, with the course of line motion achieved by controlled kinetic impulse, are the secrets of good casting.

At first reading, the rather involved technical details of the cast expounded in the chapters concerning mechanics, dynamics, and kinetics may have seemed complex and perhaps unnecessary. However, as angling adroitness increases and the basis from which to start experimentation is required, reference to these passages will prove of value to a fly fisherman who wishes to improve his skill through knowledge normally found outside the realms of angling books.

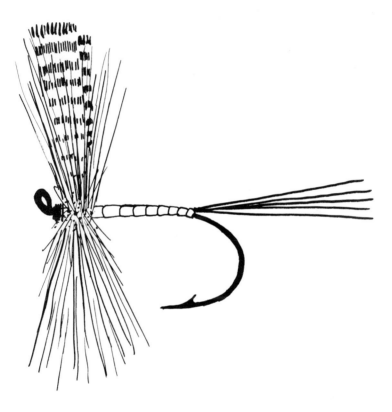

CHAPTER 6

An Analysis of the Cast

The mechanics of the cast, the dynamics of rod action, the kinetics of motion, and the energies which envelop the angling form are elements which were vaguely appreciated, although far from understood when Cotton explained the addition of extra hairs to the links of the line as it was built up towards the tip of the rod. Even in those days, it was normal practice to use a gradually tapering line with the heaviest link whipped to the uppermost section of the rod.

There is, of course, the natural resistance of air on the line and the forces of gravitational pull, but the load of the line mass, as the casting energy drives the line unfurling through the air, and the surge of kinetic impulse passing along the line — the greatest elements that infleunce fly casting performance — were certainly less tangible factors to long-ago anglers. The line tapering to the thickness of the rod tip infers that they based their principles on the whip, and, on perusal, what more natural basis was there from which to start experimentation?

I often speculate on what could have happened to fly casting if Izaak Walton and Isaac Newton had become acquainted. Their lifetimes overlapped (Newton being forty when Walton died) and Cotton and Newton were members of the same generation.

Newton's Laws of Motion apply to the act of casting as emphatically as to any other form of movement, and I trust that the tree from which falling apples dropped, to spark off his thoughts on gravity, was in view of some river in rural England.

The tapered line of Charles Cotton was known to cast better than one of level construction, although it is safe to surmise that the scientific reasons for it were not searched for, and the technological considerations lay definitely beyond that generation.

Albert Einstein introduced the Theory of Relativity. Through a stroke of genius, he added for mankind another piece of knowledge which, when applied to the angler's cast, provides greater understanding of the theory of motion. Again I hope the first germ of thought came to him near a running stream or perhaps even watching salmon leaping some waterfall.

The rod, being both a casting tool and an angling implement, has reached a point of excellence it scarcely seems possible to exceed. However, the development of new materials such as graphite filaments and carbon fibers offers a genuine 30% increase in performance from a rod half the weight of a glass-fiber rod of a similar power. The secrets of rod dynamics lie in the speed with which a rod can be moved through the air and the miniscule time factor connected with decompressional flex, a motion which adds the final thrust of energy to the line and which, with these new materials, is very much faster than the speed achieved with glass, bamboo, or metal.

Glass fiber was developed to a large extent because of the American space program, as space craft were built largely from glass fiber and resins. Fishing tackle manufacturers were on the fringe of this development (rather reminiscent of the bamboo story of World War II) and were not slow to apply new materials and technology to fishing rods. The results of ten to twenty years of normal progress were thus realized in five years.

Lines, although vastly superior to those once acknowledged as the best, will continue to improve, not only in floating and sinking ability, but also in shape (profile and weight distribution). The line described by Cotton,

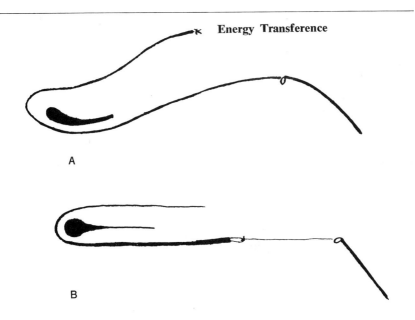

Energy Transference

A

B

A   *Shows the result of tethered impulse. Note the line dropping from the tip from the restraint of the rod. The line, robbed of kinetic momentum, falls.*

B   *Free kinetic flow. The line will normally travel until the full extension of the section occurs. It will then fall in a gliding manner.*

tapered from the thickness of the rod tip to the fly was an absolutely perfect method of achieving maximum transference of energy by the movement of the angler's cast. The motional force passes along the heavier portion of the line which, in turn, moves through a lighter section ahead and, as the energy decreases, the tapering line is in complete harmony with the dissipating force. This principle of line design — a slow, gradual taper, if applied to accuracy (dry fly) casting would improve still further the efficiency of the modern line. If such a line were paired with a progressive action rod (gradual flex produced from stress moving down the rod as more weight is exerted) it would greatly improve performance when casting up to fifty feet.

When casting a fly line, there are two different uses of the kinetic force which the angling cast generates. One is the power impulse imparted to the line when the line is trapped to the rod by the forefinger, and locked to the rod in the guides. Here the energy travels down through the line and extends it in a rolling motion. This reaction can best be described as a "tethered impulse." The other form is the free impulse, which occurs when the shooting of the line takes place. When this is performed, the impetus of the line, moving freely in the air, contains its kinetic force seated in the front of the loop, apparently dragging the lower portion of the line behind, while pulling along and turning over the upper section on its plane of travel. This is an aspect that will be better appreciated after the section devoted to the hauling technique has been examined. The hidden element of the momentum of line motion (derived from the velocity of delivery), combined with the movement of the energy which causes the mass to reverse (due to the method of propulsion) must also be taken into consideration.

A New Line Profile

A profile of the most recent development in the design of fly lines, described to me by Rod Towsley of the Berkley Company. It is basically a weight forward line to which has been added a much longer than normal tapering rear section. This type of line shape dictates that the motional behavior, within the functional tethered angling application, will out-perform similar lines in its classification (as the rear taper will tend to eliminate "drop" next to the rod tip), and will out-cast them when accepting free impulse, should the new design have the advantage of extra length and therefore additional weight. Rear tapers have been employed on the sixty-foot lines used for Tournament Salmon Distance Events for many years.

I tend to relate the Laws of Motion to rod movement, and the Theory of Relativity to line travel. Very simply, Einstein's theory explains speed related to weight: greater speed increasing the heaviness of an object (the casting of the line) and, contained within any accelerating motion, these elements create a multiple of the factor. Newton's laws are "to every action there is an equal and opposite reaction" (the compressional flex and recoil thrust of the rod) and "change of motion is proportional to the applied force and takes place in the direction of the line of force" (the plane and line of travel of the casting stroke).

LINE MANIPULATION

Now that the student has a broader appreciation of the versatility of the fly-fishing equipment he uses, and can efficiently execute the casts previously described, there are other aspects of line control and fly placement that are at his disposal.

There is, for example, the mending of line, a practice which allows the drift of the fly to be slowed or quickened to counteract the uneven flow of the current. It is done by utilizing the basic principles of the roll cast. The line is first placed upon the water and either an upstream or downstream mend is executed by making the tip of the rod throw a bag of line to the side, either up or down from the angle of line drift without affecting the initial placement of the fly.

Depositing loose line on the water by the high delivery of the cast and shaking the rod from side to side as the line extends, will form waves in the line as it falls, snaked to the surface of the water. These can range from gentle curves to pronounced bends, determined by the vigor with which the rod is waved. This is a technique used to execute a slack line cast, to place a fly normally thrown upstream to a quiet spot of water. It is left there for a longer period of time while the flow of the stream drifts the slack line, lying loosely on the surface, downstream. It can also be used to execute a natural downstream drift, although it is sometimes better practice to feed line in a downward direction by stroking it on to the surface from the rod tip, with a mend being employed to swing the fly into a spot that cannot be reached by any other method.

Adaptability is the golden rule of angling and, although the following tale is not quite in context in this section, it is nevertheless interesting and may at some time prove useful.

Many years ago I fished a certain stream where the best pool was surrounded by trees which made casting almost an impossibility and, as the banks were steep and the water too deep to wade, it was fished very little — by fly fishermen at least. The branches of the trees were placed so that there were gaps and holes in the foliage of the enclosed pool. One day I was surprised to observe a fly fisherman casting his line with his back to the water, up through a gap in the trees to his front, and making his delivery to the water on what was the backcast. After the delivery he turned and fished back his fly. I have used this method many times, throwing the line out on the backcast, and then turning to retrieve it, and have caught fish when otherwise it would have been quite impossible.

When the driving stroke of the cast is made parallel to the water and too much power is applied, the line will extend in a curve rather than on a straight course, kicking around from the side of the delivery. When insufficient force is used for the delivery stroke, the line will not extend fully and the curve of the line will lie to the side that originated the stroke.

These styles are used for drifting the dry fly or for nymphing in the surface film. The advantages of these casts over the conventional snaking deposit created by waving the rod tip are occasionally superior. Of one thing I am certain, Tommy Edwards might have accepted the terms over-energized and under-powered, but I am sure he would have had some electrifying comments on negative and positive casts.

It is a fact that a much lighter presentation of the fly can be achieved more often with a slicing cast made from a plane level with the water (like the forehand drive in tennis), although the degree of accuracy with this cast is vastly inferior to the overhead method.

When the rod is held low to the water, the full extended length of the line is influenced by the flow of the water and the line drags in the current which is a necessary element of sunk-fly fishing.

For dry-fly fishing, the rod is held high to avoid drag, keeping as much of the line off the water as possible. Drag is the effect of the water flow on the line. Sometimes it can be an advantage and at other times an infernal nuisance. It is possible to pick the line from the water with a "snake" pickup, done by shaking the rod from side to side and causing waves of energy to pass down the line which break the line free of the grip of surface tension and allow it to be lifted clear of the water without submerging the fly on lift off. The command of line tension, the regulation of line behavior, and the control of line placement achieved by rod manipulation can defeat the influence of the movement of the current upon the line and the presentation of the fly.

CASTING WITH THE TWO-HANDED ROD

Casting a fly line with a two-handed fly rod is today used almost exclusively for Atlantic Salmon fishing, although in some European countries double-handed rods are used for trout fishing in lakes and on larger rivers.

The long, twin-handed fly-casting rod has a use in salmon fly fishing, as a long line can be cast consistently with little effort, hour after hour without fatigue. This task, if performed with a proper single-handed rod, would entail a great deal of line stripping, false casting, and line shooting, and prove to be a tiring business.

For salmon angling, two-handed rods are usually from ten to fourteen feet in length and are contained within Classes Seven to Twelve (power assessments). Two hands are used to grip the long rod handle (the fishing reel is situated between the hands), but it is the uppermost hand which performs the casting function and the lower hand supports the weight of the rod. Because of the length of the rod, there is less forearm movement used in the casting action (it becomes a short, accelerating pulling and pushing motion) and the lifting wrist action is emphasized.

After the required amount of line has been extended on to the water, the rod is held with the dominant hand gripping the handle at shoulder level, and the secondary hand supporting the base of the butt by either cupping the rubber button in the palm, or by holding the lowest portion of the handle at a point close to the midriff. The reel is attached to the rod between the hands and the line is trapped to the handle by the uppermost hand in the same manner as was employed for the single-handed cast.

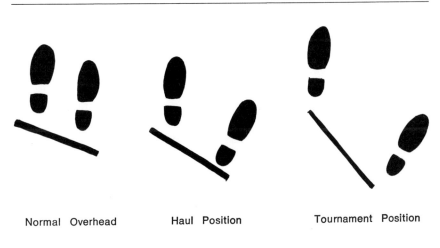

Normal Overhead   Haul Position   Tournament Position

Feet and Shoulder Positions for Fly Casting

The best way to become familiar with the two-handed fly rod is to practise the roll cast. The butt of the rod is stationed close to the body, dictating that the uppermost hand must execute a shorter forward push and wrist turn in a positive motion to roll out the line for a clean turnover.

To perform the lift-off into the aerialized cast, the upper hand moves out to a position at the front, to two-thirds of the reach that it is possible to extend from the body, while the lower hand is hugged close to the midriff. With the single-handed cast, the first motion was forearm lift. When a double-handed rod is used, the movement is an accelerating pulling-back motion, culminated with an upward flick of the wrist that is achieved more

101

decisively by the lower hand swinging out from the body at a distance of four or five inches (as though the rod had a pivot through it at a point midway between the hands). Old-time instructors taught the movement (or rather the limitations of the motion) by undoing the lowest button of the pupil's waistcoat and anchoring the little finger of the lower hand in the button hole.

It should be stressed that the casting action of the two-handed rod must not be hurried. The longer rod must be given time to react to the cast and a longer period allowed for the line to extend. As it is extending, the student may turn his head and watch the line unfurl to the rear. The frontal delivery is executed by first pushing forward with the dominant arm and, as the wrist action is applied, pulling the butt of the rod into the body with the lower hand which tucks in just below the rib cage. This rather scissor-like casting stroke has the effect of tipping the rod forward, the longer rod taking more time to react to the motion and the slower recovery flexure giving the impression of a very leisurely casting action.

During this course of instruction, the rod has been held roughly upright to the body, tilted at a slight angle out from the shoulder over which the cast was made. This casting position will achieve the normal delivery of line. However, if a low driving delivery of the line is required (for the roll or the aerialized cast), the angle of the rod across the body must be made more pronounced, with the lower hand located at a point out to the side of the ribs. This allows a much lower stroke of the rod to be made by the upper hand. The bottom hand finishes the cast at a position next to the hip.

Correct use of the long rod makes easy work of casting. It is quite a simple procedure to alternate the position of the hands gripping the rod to efficiently execute the cast from either side of the body (the dominant hand always being involved). Right hand uppermost from that side of the trunk; and the left hand above to throw the line from that side of the body.

Shooting the line is done in the same manner as was described for the single-handed cast. Casting can also be done "cross handed," a method which can be applied to single-handed casting by using the right hand to cast over the left shoulder, or the line thrown over the right shoulder by the left hand. The correct methods are usually better, although circumstances may occasionally govern their use.

In Britain when salmon fly fishing was still in its infancy, the two-handed rod was constructed to float as well as cast a fly for, when a large fish was hooked and all the line had been taken from the reel, the complete outfit was thrown into the river and retrieved from the tail of the pool hopefully with the salmon still attached, after it had exhausted itself pulling around eighteen feet of timber.

To see a two-handed rod used properly is to witness an angling delight: it is undoubtedly the supreme tool for the task of salmon fishing, especially when angling from a boat or where the casting of a constant length of line

102

is required, when large flies are being cast, good presentation of the fly is required at long distances, long mends of line essential for success, or when the positive control of a hooked fish is necessary. It is a fine piece of fishing equipment, and occupies an illustrious niche in the history of angling.

THE DOUBLE HAUL

The ability to cast much greater distances than can be attained by the single-hand method of casting is a tremendous advantage to the modern fly fisherman. The tournament technique of hauling is now an accepted procedure among those of the angling fraternity who require more positive control of the tackle or demand maximum performance from their equipment.

The double-haul technique (casting mechanics) increases the speed of the line (kinetic velocity) and extracts greater flexural force (dynamic impulse) from the rod. When combined, these elements result in a much higher level of casting performance.

The hauling method of casting involves the secondary hand, working in harmony with the front and rear motion of the rod. The free hand tugs on the line as the casting rhythm of the dominant hand applies the final surge of power with each delivery stroke, to front and rear, and then feeds the line recovered back as the rod "drifts" and adopts a position next to the rod hand, ready for the next haul upon the line.

It is the still-water anglers, the salt-water fly casters, and the big-river fishermen who have embraced the tourney technique in their fishing styles. In some instances the lake angler uses a shooting taper line with monofilament backing (although fine-diameter floating running line is, I find, more practical than monofilament) to cover as much water as possible. The salt-water caster employs heavy, steep-taper, weight-forward lines to push out the large flies that are used for his sport, and the wide-river fisherman naturally wishes to reach as far across the river as possible.

Any standard fly-fishing outfit can be made to produce a fifty per cent better casting performance (when only one hand has been used to cast the line) by the use of the hauling method. However, it must be established that unless the caster can use his equipment efficiently in the normal angling manner, the more complex mechanics of the double haul will be beyond him.

The hauling technique is not difficult to learn. I choose to teach the method on grass, in order that the two directional motions and the actions they contain can be taught separately.

When a double-tapered line is being used, I have the pupil stand with the maximum amount of line that can be handled, extended to the front of

Casting with the two-handed fly rod . . .

the caster. Should a weight-forward line be employed, the full length of the heavy section of the line, plus three feet of the running line, should be extended from the tip of the rod to the ground.

The double-haul technique requires that the secondary hand be used to tug on the line at specific instants during the cast and feed out line at other periods. The first half of the cast is executed by the dominant hand in the same manner as is done for the normal overhead cast. However, included in the motion is the secondary hand, before the start of the movement, gripping the line (which was somewhat similar to the position adopted when the lesson on the shooting of extra line was given) alongside the hand holding the rod. As the rod is raised by forearm lift, the hand gripping the line is held close to the rod hand and, as the wrist action is applied, the secondary hand pulls quickly down and back.

. . . alternating hand positions.

These two actions in unison throw the line back on the rearward flight at a much faster speed than can be produced when only one hand is involved and, as the rod tilts in the decelerating drift to the rear, the secondary hand is lifted back to the position next to the rod hand.

The momentum of the line traveling to the rear should pull the complete section being used tight to the haul hand, and keep it fully taut on extension, where it is allowed to fall to the ground.

The angler does an about face and practises the first half of the cast until the haul-hand motion finds the right co-ordination and is integrated into the movement. The duty of the haul hand is to add sufficient speed to the line, on the haul, for the aerialized section, as it turns over to the rear, to contain enough energy (receive adequate velocity) to draw after it the line which was fed back when the haul hand was raised alongside the rod hand.

105

Let me say at this point that the casting act I am attempting to describe is better appreciated when it is seen and if the adage one picture is worth a thousand words is right, the physical act is worth ten thousand. When the synchronization of the first part of the cast has been learned, and the angler can produce the necessary amount of speed to pull the line taut, and the secondary hand lifted automatically up to the position next to the hand which holds the rod, the second half of the haul can be taught.

With the line extended to the rear of the caster, a forward delivery is made. Again the rod hand executes the same motions as when the normal overhead cast is done. The movements performed by the secondary hand inside the motion are first a travel path alongside the dominant hand and, at the instant that the wrist action which drives the line to the front is applied by the rod hand, the secondary hand gives a vigorous downward pull on the line. This tug is taken to the maximum extension of the arm and then the haul hand moves up to the position next to the rod hand. The action should impart sufficient forward velocity to the aerialized section of line to pull the complete length of line taut to the haul hand. An about face places the caster in the position to keep repeating the exercise until the second half of the casting technique can be done properly and the timing of the hauling motion is correct. The essential factor in learning the haul action is line speed. Unless the line is pulled taut to the hand on extension by the velocity of motion, the haul movement is nullified and very little is added to the cast.

When both the rearward and frontal single haul actions are integrated into the separate fore and aft casting movements, which up to this point have been learnt individually, the caster is ready to put the complete double haul together in the aerialized cast. I find that by using this method of instruction, the complexities of the tournament technique are learnt without too much difficulty.

The stance required for the hauling action is more open than that used for the normal overhead cast. The back foot is turned out, and is placed more to the rear, the shoulders are turned more, with the delivery arm well behind the front foot. Body weight is evenly distributed over both feet.

In fly-distance competitions the stance is more crouched with feet farther apart and the knees bent, and there is a subtle transference of weight from rear to front on the forward delivery, and from front to rear on the back-cast. This weight shift is done very smoothly inside the casting action and is a nuance that is difficult to detect unless the onlooker is aware that it is happening.

The haul technique applied to still-water fly fishing to obtain extra distance, at the Greenbank Trout Club, Ontario. Here the forward motion of the cast shows the secondary hand pulling the line downwards to add greater velocity to the delivery.

The Movements of the Double Haul

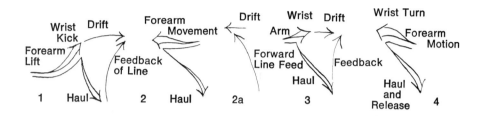

Fig. 1   Shows the actions of the hands going into the backcast

Figs. 2 and 2a   The hand motions for the forward delivery

Fig. 3   The movements into the backcast

Fig. 4   Actions for the final delivery

Drift action and feedback of line prevent the line nearest the tip of the rod from falling (the section which received the kinetic impulse first, and which the motivational force has passed along would fall when robbed of the momentum of the cast). However, by allowing a slight amount of travel (the drift and feed are sufficient to eliminate this tendency), the angler is kept in perfect contact with the line.

The angle of the haul, dictated by the accelerating course taken by the secondary hand, can be anywhere from a stabbing down-and-back motion, to an outward-flinging arm motion to the side, with the fingers stretched to their limits to add an inch or so to the most distal course of travel. The object in the haul is to recover as much line as possible back through the guides to speed the line. Choose whichever style of hauling method suits you best. It should be noted that when fishing waist deep in the water, unless the side pull is used, the downward method will place the hand at the limit of extension into the water and, although this may not matter when the angler is fly casting for bonefish under sunny skies, a soaked fishing jacket arm when throwing flies for winter steelhead is to be avoided.

When using a shooting head (shooting taper) always attach the heaviest monofilament it is practical to employ, as the elasticity of the material can be the cause of poor performance by stretching at the point of maximum impulse from the resistance of the line, and so rob the casting stroke of velocity. This condition will occur if too fine a strength of monofilament is used for running line (under the misapprehension that the lighter line test will cast farther), and there is the likelihood of erratic transfer of kinetic energy which will cause tremors in the line that create a poor delivery and produce an equally bad extension.

The tournament hauling technique is a most interesting casting movement. The complete body of the caster is involved at some stage of the cast: both arms, one pulling and feeding the line, the other pushing and pulling the rod. The shoulders, trunk, and legs blend into the timing, adding to the power impulse and lending themselves advantageously to the mechanics of the cast.

It is the grip on the rod, the flexor and extensor muscles of the forearm, the bicep, triceps, deltoid, pectoral, and shoulder girdle of the casting arm, plus the corresponding muscle groups of the hauling arm that execute the bulk of the work, although the rest of the body contributes to the rhythm of the power flow.

Without any doubt, the mastery of the double haul for single-handed casting increases the angling potential of the fly fisherman. It takes practice, certainly, but once adequate line speed can be generated to provide sufficient velocity to enable the hauling hand to feel the line pull on extension, and so allow the haul action to be executed in a positive manner, dimensions of line control and casting distance open up that were previously unattainable. Ten to twenty yards of shooting line can be cast behind a shooting taper, making practical angling casts of over thirty-five yards quite possible.

Casting a shooting head, attached to monofilament backing, is an exhilarating experience and provides a new dimension to angling. Distances cast in competition with specialized equipment are quite staggering: over 69 yards for the trout event (one hand) and over 80 yards for the salmon competition (two hands). It is an aspect of angling that was developed by the Golden Gate Casting Club for fly-distance events in the late 1940's.

Over the years, numerous angling pundits, after witnessing a casting tournament for the first time, recognize the virtues of the technique and immediately recommend that anglers start cutting up a line, attaching monofilament and, by so doing, at once achieve great casting potential. Nothing is further from the truth. Even if the angler can cast well initially, without knowledge of the mechanics of the hauling technique he will be unable to master the line and will have a most frustrating and disillusioning experience, one that will sour his taste for casting tournaments and cause a subconscious resentment towards tourney casters — instead of the feeling being directed at the ill-informed writer who gave him the information.

Cutting a fly line is a serious business and should not be undertaken without guidance or good advice. Should any reader be sufficiently interested, the best idea is to buy the most inexpensive level line classified to the rod power to be used, cut it at a point of maximum control, plus three feet, attach it to a thirty-pound length of monofilament, and start practising. Use the diagram of the haul hand motions for reference, and base the exercise on the two-part instruction method described earlier. Done this way, the angler can learn as he goes along, getting a better grasp of the subject and drawing his own conclusions.

109

Possibly Don Neish, the London tackle dealer, and myself (because of our connections and positions in the British tackle industry at that time) cut more lines to pieces during our early tournament days than fifty avid anglers would use in a lifetime.

The basics are that a line must have a tapering, wedge-like profile and the longer it is — naturally providing the line can be controlled in the air and delivered correctly — the farther it will travel.

Our last dual effort of line building was several years ago when our casting enthusiasm was at its zenith. It consisted of lengths of high-density lines cut from double-tapered lines Classes 6, 7, 8, 9, 10, that measured 51 feet and weighed a fraction under 1½ ounces, and was used on an 8-ounce, 8-foot 9-inch fast taper rod that was analyzed as 75% lever and 25% spring. I still have this tackle today and, being mellowed by the trials of experience, consider that good technique is more likely to be productive in the long run than the elusive search for new and better equipment — although I am as susceptible as the rest, where tackle is concerned. . .

During the early sixties at one of the British Casting Association Tournaments at Scarborough, the final event to be cast was the two-handed salmon fly distance. The wind was blowing a gale, shooting line was impossible to place and was blown into the lake from the casting platforms. The lake at times looked like the North Sea and, although at first appraisal it seemed that a record cast would be produced because of the advantageous conditions of the strong wind blowing to the front, there was the problem of putting the line back into the teeth of the gale, before it could be brought forward and released to ride on the wind to the front.

The majority of casters were men in the prime of life, with a scattering of the old timers who looked as though the wind might blow them away. The result of the event was quite a revelation. First, second, and third were Lionel Sweet, Tommy Edwards, and Pierre Creusevaut — the youngest of them was over sixty and the oldest over seventy years of age! If ever a situation proved emphatically the value of experience over youthful enthusiasm, it was seeing the winners at that event. It showed very clearly that finesse and experience are vastly superior to strength without expertise.

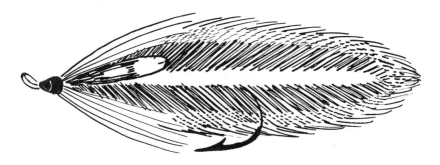

CHAPTER 7

The Take

Before entering into the method and technique of angling with a fly, there is the most important aspect of the sport, the awareness of which will increase the fisherman's prospects of success — the *take*. When the feathered offering is taken, the action is described as a *rise* if the fly is taken at the surface. It is called a *strike* when taken under the water and, in both instances, the angler *tightens on* by drawing the line taut to the fish and hooking it.

The strike may also be applicable to the action made when drawing the line tight to the fish, but to avoid any confusion, the word "strike" will only be applied to the motion of the fish taking the fly sub-surface. There was a similar situation in fishing terminology not too long ago with the word "cast," which could mean either the act of casting or — as it is now known — the leader, which is a better definition. Unless the fisherman is fully aware of exactly what is happening when the take occurs, we have a situation as frustrating to the angler as to the indoor-taught casters on their first visit to a stream.

The surface rise is a feeding action which is easily detected by the disturbance created by the fish taking food forms either in, or near, the surface film or actually on the water. Dealing first with the acceptance of the floating offering, it will be discovered that a great amount of instinctive timing has to be developed which can only come from practical experience. However, there is certain basic information which can be divulged that will prove of immense value.

As a rule, the larger a fish, the slower and more ponderous will be its rise to the fly. The rise is an aspect of dry-fly work that normally leaves anglers new to the technique in a quandary: they find that they can cast well enough to lay the line positively yet delicately upon the water, control drift and drag, dictate the position and movement of the fly on the current, and even have the fish accept it, but the actual hooking of the fish causes great problems.

Invariably the angler will jerk the rod up and pull the fly away from the fish as soon as the surface of the water is seen to be broken by the action of the rise. Occasionally there is reversal of this predicament and the angler does nothing at all, which allows the fish time to detect the unedible nature of the steel and feather morsel and eject it. What occurs when a fish takes food from the surface film or off the surface is that the fly is approached by the fish at an upward tilted angle and a scooping motion is made as the nose is pushed above the fly, allowing the water to be sucked into the maw, carrying along with it the selected item of food. There is then a downward tipping movement of the fish coinciding with the closing of the jaw, the gills being used to eject water and air and the throat is opened to swallow the food. There are times when a rise occurs and it proves such a deliberate feeding action that too fast a tightening on by the fly fisherman will draw the fly away from the fish. On other occasions, the fly is ejected more quickly than the angler can react to the rise and tighten the line to make contact with the fish. This subject will be discussed in more detail in the section dealing specifically with dry-fly fishing.

I am convinced that fish are fully aware of every happening within the liquid environment which, let us not forget, is their domain. That they can detect color and form is undeniable. However, with the minute band of sensory capacity they have, their reactions to danger and feeding stimulus are based to a great extent on the imitative process of learning and are contained within the natural instinct for survival (tiny fish in a hatchery see the more mature fish feeding and imitate the motion). Intelligence as we know it does not apply to the quarry of the angler, although at times it would seem that angling becomes a battle of wits, with the dejected fisherman in the role of the vanquished, and the war lost to a creature without the power to reason!

It is essential at this juncture to deal briefly with light refraction and the limitations of a cone-shaped field of vision endowed by nature to the denizens of the water world. Because of the cone-shaped window, the closer a fish is to the surface, the more tilted and narrow is the field of observation and, when it rises to a fly, at the final instant of the take it loses sight of the object. It is generally accepted that a fish first detects the floating insect by light patterns, rather than by the perception of form and should there be a feeding impulse stimulated by size, shape, shade, or the shimmer of movement when the feathered offering of the angler is accepted, only the upper portion of the fly (the wing or hackles) can be seen as the feeding motion occurs.

Underwater visual conditions are quite extraordinary when a fish is viewing the surface for food. There is the cone-shaped window of vision, the angle of refraction, light pattern, stream movement, and a reverse mirror situation of the river bed. If the fish is stimulated to take food from the surface, the elements of angle, speed, visual adjustment, and distance are quite complex. (Through human eyes and reasoning, at least!)

This subject is covered in great detail by Vincent Marinaro in his book *A Modern Dry Fly Code*, and should any reader wish to explore it further, this book is to be recommended.

What the fish actually sees is a matter of conjecture. However there are certain guidelines which are certainly worth mentioning and thinking about. The gossamer fragility and color tones of the natural insect, the minute features and coloration of an aquatic creature, or the delicate form and shade of small bait fish are far removed from the silk and feather-dressed fly of the angler. Regardless of the perfection of the tie, and the quality of

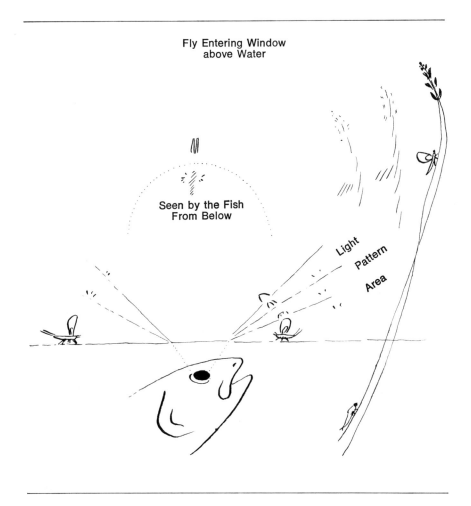

Fly Entering Window
above Water

Seen by the Fish
From Below

Light
Pattern
Area

the materials used, it is far short of the creature it is supposed to imitate. It is completely alien to the natural object it simulates simply because of the hook upon which it is constructed.

To a great extent success depends not on what is being fished, but how it is fished, providing the size and color are somewhat similar to the food upon which the fish are feeding. This is carried even further when fly patterns that have no counterparts in nature, and are simply attractors, catch fish.

Many years ago A. J. McClane wrote an article, that for me put the subject of fly type, color, and style into perspective, the title of which was "Suggestion or Perfect Imitation." The pertinent theme was that a suggestive fly of a reasonable likeness in shape and color to the natural it is meant to represent and more importantly, if it is used in a stimulative manner, is really all that is required. A theory which, I may add, can be applied to all forms of fly fishing.

The Cone-Shaped Field
of Vision with the Stream
Bed Mirrored in the Surface

Fly Reflected
in Surface Film

In still water or in a slow-moving stream the rise to the floating insect (where the fly is scooped from the surface rather than plucked from the surface film) is normally a deliberate feeding action and the fly fisherman tightens on. When there is little or no current flow, the fish will unhurriedly approach the fly, examining it as it draws near and will either accept it or reject it. In fast water when casts are being made at an upstream angle there is much less time for the fish to examine the fly and the feeding action in flowing water is much faster, which dictates a speedier tighten-on. In all conditions, of course, allowance must be made for the amount of slack line deposited on the water which must be taken up in order to be in contact with the fish from the rod tip.

There is another visual rise form that an angler will encounter which is produced when fish are feeding on food deposited in, or just under, the surface film. These edible items can be either emerging nymphs or spent insects. When nymphs are the object, the fish will be seen to dart around and feed busily, producing a bulging type of rise. The feeding action with spent insects is more leisurely and produces the classic dimple rise. As a rule, fish move quickly to an edible item that may escape (such as a nymph) and will adopt a quite casual approach to creatures trapped in the surface film (a spent insect).

The dimple rise form provides the fly fisherman with a really tough problem, as this feeding effect always takes place towards dusk when the larger fish come out of hiding and start to forage for food. A six-inch and a six-pound fish create the same disturbance as an exhausted and waterlogged fly is sipped through the surface. A slow tightening of the line is the best advice under these circumstances, while with the faster bulging rise form (which technically is a sub-surface strike), a fish is rarely missed by the angler.

Slack line, surface drag, water speed, the size of the fish, and the quickness of the feeding action are all contributing factors to the angler hooking a fish that rises to the fly (as is the angle at which the rod is moved). One thing I do know, and that is that an angler who has his reflexes sharpened to tighten on fast enough to hook four and six-inch fish will be too quick with larger fish, and will pull the fly away from them or break the leader tippet.

Unlike the rise, the take under the water, the sub-surface strike, is detected by feel and, unless the line is taut from the rod to the fly, the feathered deceiver can be taken and ejected with the angler left completely oblivious of the fact that the fly has been accepted and rejected.

When the fly is taken below the surface on a taut line (the fly and leader in contact with the line: the line with the tip and, from the tip, the rod transmitting awareness to the hand) and when the strike is detected, the fish has already taken the fly. Often with larger fish, the tightening-on motion to set the hook is not necessary, the fish having hooked itself when it took the fly.

The strike can vary from the most gentle of plucks made by the fish at slow-moving nymphs and sensed through the rod tip to a rod-arching, butt-jerking, wrist-straining jolt when a large fish smashes at a fast-retrieved streamer fly. Underwater feeding movements range from a lazy forward nibble to a veritable slashing sideways attack and, as a rule, the angler will react with an instinctive corresponding motion.

Should fish be repeatedly lost because of a poor hook hold, it may possibly be the fault of an over-light tightening of the equipment or too large a hook on a light outfit (check for a blunt or barbless hook). Continual breaks on the strike can be caused by too powerful a wrist action, a strong rod being used with light poundage leaders (although it could be attributable to wind knots in the tippet caused by too early a forward delivery of the line when casting). Normally with the tightening-on method, which draws an already-taut line tighter to the rod creating a positive connection of the fly to the quarry, the weight of the fish drives home the barb. A line tight to the rod casts well, and a line taut to the hook catches fish.

MANIPULATING THE FLY

The rod is both a casting tool and a casting implement and the fly is manipulated through it, after the line has been cast. It can be done either upon the surface by subtle twitching movements of the tip which produce minute flickers of motion, to a positive skating action to induce a rise. Also the underwater presentation, from a slow faltering return to a darting erratic retrieve that provokes a strike, and the materials from which a fly is made, all contribute greatly to the action the feathered offering produces when fished by the fly angler.

The object of fly fishing is to place and manipulate the fly with the rod

116

and line, on or under the water in a manner which attracts the fish and creates sufficient interest or sparks a feeding stimulus strong enough to induce the take.

Some of the more conventional of the present-day flies must no doubt bear a close resemblance to the patterns described in *The Book of St. Albans,* although recent years have seen a complete departure from traditional materials and quite startling developments in style and form. This, together with better equipment, has broadened the spectrum of the fly tremendously. The modern line in particular has made the wet fly much more productive and has created new methods of fly fishing. Line design has made possible greater casting distances.

A fly treated with floatant and fished upon the surface of the water with a floating line is generally meant to represent a natural insect which can be a product of either land or water (mayflies and caddis are deemed "dry flies," and crickets and ants, "terrestials," in modern nomenclature). Some of these artificial flies bear no relation to any natural thing, yet are very successful fish producers, which again emphasizes the point that it is not what is being used, but how it is being fished that matters. Flies fished in the surface film, using either a floating line or one of intermediate density, can be meant to imitate hatching, drowned, or water-logged insects; and shallow-fished wet flies that suggest aquatic life forms; or streamer flies that simulate bait fish, take a fair percentage of the season's fish. The line densities now available to the fly fisherman allow flies to be fished in even the deepest of water with great success, because of their unique control, sinking, slow sinking, fast sinking, and extra fast-sinking qualities.

The wet fly must be fished in such a way as to attract fish, and the dry fly must be presented in a natural manner. In moving water the current plays an important role. The wet fly is cast across the water flow and allowed to swing back while the rod is twitched or rocked to enable the materials from which it is made to simulate life. However, the dry fly must be maneuvered with the initial placement of the line so as to drift naturally on the surface. In some cases the line must be repositioned as it moves with the flow to permit the travel path of the fly to occur as normally as the water-borne journey of the natural insect would be.

Under the water the fly can be fished at all speeds of recovery. In moving water the current assists the action, but in still water the angler must supply the fishing movement. Subaqueous recoveries vary from the tiniest of teasing twitches to fast, jabbing stabs; from the stillest and most placid of drifts, to realistically-applied fluttering and skating movements.

CHAPTER 8

More on Equipment and Technique

EQUIPMENT

Let us assume that the angler is now approaching the stage when suitable tackle will have to be selected and we shall cover again very briefly what has already been laid down as being a reasonably sound basis from which to start, and slightly broaden some of the original comments.

We have discussed the basic equipment, and have related the size of the fly to be cast to the power of the outfit to be used, and allowed the physical angling conditions to dictate the length of the rod. There is, of course, the selection of line, its type and shape, to be made. For a first choice, purchase a floating line. It can be argued that in some situations a sinking line would perhaps be best. However, operating within the limitations of only one line, the floater is the most sensible investment, as it enables one to both surface fish, and, should circumstances demand it, a longer leader with a heavy fly can be employed to present the offering at lower depths. A double-tapered line would be my own recommendation for line Class Six and below, and a weight forward for line Class Seven and above. My advice is similar for sink-tip lines, and weight forward is my personal choice of line for any of the line classes in sinking lines.

Ideally, an angler should fish with a rod which has matched to it three reels — or one reel with two extra spools — carrying floating, sinking, and sink-tip lines: with these he can fish confidently and angle competently on any stretch of water, because he can use all the recognized fly-fishing techniques that these lines are capable of performing.

A good selection of flies for the type of fish in the area that is to be visited is essential and care must be taken to ensure that they are the correct

Here is a cross-section of the variety of flies and attractors that are available to the modern fly fisherman.

size and the accepted patterns used by the resident population of fly fishermen. From my experience, local knowledge is always a tremendous help, and only a fool would ignore information of this kind. Although it can occasionally be proved wrong, I never start off by trying to show that another method of fishing or a different approach is better. Finally, leaders and tippets of a strength relative to the bulk of the fly are needed.

An angling vest is a wise investment, as the numerous pockets eliminate the necessity of carrying a fishing bag. The vest can hold many items of the fly fisherman's equipment, such as dry-fly floatant, leader sink liquid, line dressing (I still use Aspinall's Mucilin in the red tin which, incidentally, does not have a harmful effect on modern floating lines), nylon clippers, thermometer, tippet coils, polarized glasses, fly boxes, insect repellant, spare reels or spools, a lightweight waterproof of some kind, and some roomy pocket in which to carry a snack. It is always wise to carry a large pin to clear varnish-filled hook eyes, and to unpick the occasional wind knot in a leader. The angling vest is an accepted part of the fly fisherman's image, and its tremendous usefulness is undeniable. The design of the fishing vest was pioneered by Lee Wulff, an American with an international angling reputation.

A hat to protect the head from the elements (invariably with a degree of individuality and character), where flies can be placed to dry off; waders, either hip or chest height; a landing net of adequate size, a fish tailer, or gaff are necessary.

Line Function in Swift Water

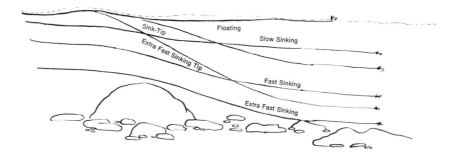

TECHNIQUE

When playing a fish, after the initial hooking,the rod is held at a 45-degree angle and the fish is played against the drag of the reel with the curve of the rod used to keep tension on the fish at all times. The spring of the rod and the check of the reel eventually wear down the energy of the fish. When possible, it is best to get below a fish, where there is the combined force of the flexed rod, the restraint of the reel, and the pull of the current to tire the fish. Should the fish jump, the tip of the rod should be lowered to eliminate the possibility of the fish striking the leader and breaking the tippet by giving it an instant of slack line. In old-time salmon fishing parlance "salute the salmon and bow to the leaping fish" is excellent advice.

When landing a fish, the piscine opponent should be led over the submerged net which is raised to trap the hooked quarry. It is not good practice to scoop at the fish hoping to enmesh it, as the action invariably startles the fish into making another attempt at escape. If a tailer is being used, the fish must be played out and steadied with the rod before the wire snare is slipped over the tail and lifted. The gaff, which is employed for large fish, is normally used by an assistant and, with care, can be hooked into the bony part of the jaw without damaging the fish. The hook is then removed, and the fish released none the worse from its encounter with the fly fisherman.

We are aware that the rod is both a casting tool and a fishing implement, and have developed the necessary skills to use the equipment efficiently . . . . We understand the basics of casting: the mechanics, dynamics, and kinetics involved in the placement of the line and the positioning of the fly, as well as the requirements of presentation: a line tight to the rod casts well and a line taut to the fly catches fish . . . . It is not what is being caught that decides the strength of the outfit, but what is to be cast . . . The rudiments of casting remain constant regardless of the casting plane, or the angle of line travel . . .There is a better appreciation of the fishing fly, and how it should be fished. We must not forget the theory of suggestion rather than exact imitation, and fish accordingly . . . The rod can be used to manipulate the fly and by its action transmit "life" to the feathered offering to a degree which can control success or failure . . . We know of the fundamentals of the take; the rise and the strike, and the tighten on . . . .

The fly can be an attempt of insect imitation or simply an attractor pattern. Dressings, tied on fine steel hooks, are the product of the imagination and flair of the tier and are made from all manner of materials. Stiff cock hackles and other fibers, furs and hair with good flotation are used for dry flies, as opposed to wet flies for which the fly dresser uses soft feathers and absorbent body materials; hair tied at an angle to "kick" when used in fast water; soft marabou feathers that produce a "breathing" action in still water; bunches of colored hackles that work in a squid-like motion for salt-water species. Combinations of stiff or soft feathers, resilient hair, translucent fur, tinsels, silks, wool, and synthetics in unending colors, combine and contribute to the attractiveness of the fly and, when allied with the intelligent use of the rod, can prove to be deadly. What a fish actually sees when the fly is presented, what motivational reaction is generated by the feathered offering, and what exactly stimulates the take is a matter of speculation.

Whether it be a seven-inch speckled trout in some tiny creek, or a seventy-pound tarpon in a saltwater bay; scrappy sunfish in a lake, or the mighty salmon in some brawling river; the thrill is the same, with the fisherman deriving similar pleasures, enjoying the same feelings of elation, and savoring the sport to its fullest.

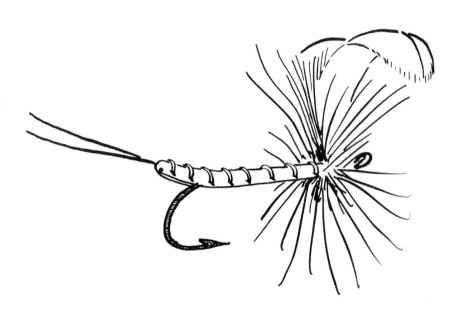

CHAPTER 9

Wading: Equipment and Technique

EQUIPMENT

At this point, a brief word regarding wading is necessary. The use of hip or chest waders is most advantageous, as they allow the angler to cover water that ordinarily would not be within casting distance. There are various types of materials used in the manufacture of wading apparel — rubber latex, plastic, canvas and rubber-faced cotton or rubberized nylon, as well as other synthetics. Most have the boot part of the foot attached, although some are made with a stocking-foot leg which necessitates wearing a wading brogue or sandal over them. There are many on the market, and the only advice I can offer is to obtain the best quality that the pocket will allow, for it will be found that the more expensive the item, the better it will perform and last. Waders with a studded or felt sole offer a much safer footing than those with a rubber-cleated bottom. Canvas is the coolest of the materials to wear in warm weather. Lightweight materials are less fatiguing to walk around in and there are on the market insulated waders for angling in low temperatures.

I find it best to use over-large chest waders, as they allow the air to circulate in hot weather, and leave space for extra clothing under cold conditions. A jacket may be worn inside the top if deep wading is necessary. The additional length gained in the legs, although not enhancing one's appearance, does give additional freedom of movement. If the leg cannot be lifted to a height which enables the foot to be placed on the seat of a chair, they are too short in the leg.

To negotiate large, fast-flowing rivers safely, a wading staff is a wise investment. An inflatable angling vest, or a buoyancy jacket are essential if really deep and torrential streams are to be fished.

On smaller bodies of water, casts can be made from a kneeling position in the stream and in heavily wooded areas, waders offer great advantages when making progress either upstream or down, in the water course itself.

TECHNIQUE

There are rules which must be observed when wading: in a strong current always offer only one side of the body to the force of the water when changing position or use a crab-like gait, digging the heels into the river bed to make progress. Never attempt to step over boulders. Move around them, as there is the high risk of a fall when one leg is lifted to straddle a large, slippery stone, and the restricted degree of movement allowed by waders should never be forgotten. If an about face must be made, do it facing downstream and at all costs avoid getting into a "crossed leg" position, a situation which creates imbalance. Think out every move before attempting any maneuver and, if a rest is necessary, turn and lean on the flow and attempt to angle the course of the wade with the current rather than against it. Never panic. If a fall occurs relax, and go with the stream feet first, steering towards the safest bank.

There is a fallacy concerning a fall while wearing chest waders — anglers believe that air trapped inside the waders will turn the fisherman upside down. This is not so. Should the angler be wading in waist-deep water, all the air is forced out of the wading apparel by the pressure of the water (anyone who has waded can recall the press of the water flow on the legs and trunk), and a fall in any depth results in the waders filling with water. The imperative thing to remember is to go with the current, feet first. Keep a clear head and think out the situation. Invariably, when a footing is once more achieved, it will be discovered that the rod is still grasped and, in most cases, held above the head for safety during the impromptu journey.

Avoid sections of a river where there is too much danger involved to attempt wading it (above fierce rapids and falls, and immediately upstream of deep current-torn pools). Believe me, there is no angling venue that can justify sport to the degree when such involvement holds the risk to life and limb!

A companion of mine, a top-flight European salmon fisherman, when fishing a certain Scottish river, used to tie a stout mountaineering rope around his waist, anchor the rope firmly to a boulder, and lower himself down difficult runs of the stream. This practice allowed him to cast and present his fly — and take fish — from spots that were ignored by other fishermen because of the rocks and the gushing flow of water. He used the rope to steady himself in the strong current. It was an invaluable help to retrace his steps back to shore. It is a practice which I do not recommend, unless the angler has a companion on the bank stationed to observe his progress and to help him back to shore. It is really quite strange to discover that a hooked salmon, for example, can have a tremendous steadying effect to the wading fisherman, enabling the angler to follow the fish, and cross quite fast sections of water safely.

The possession of wading apparel, to the majority of anglers, seems to give them license to enter the water at every opportunity without giving the matter any thought whatsoever. There is more to fishing than simply getting waders wet. On smaller streams it is best to stay out of the water whenever possible. Consider what happens when the angler enters the water: the smaller denizens of the stream scatter in frightened flight, which alarms the larger bait fishes into startled movement. That, in turn, results in a chain reaction of fear, alertness, and caution throughout the whole area which puts the larger fish on guard — if they have not already departed for the safety of some hidden lair.

Never walk along the bank showing a silhouette clearly against the light. Move slowly. Should the stream have to be waded, move with deliberate stealth and avoid causing undue disturbance. If necessary, wait quite motionless after the desired position has been reached to allow the scared activities of the smallest residents of the stream to abate, and let the larger inhabitants regain composure. Watch the water and, if the telltale ripple of your advance is pronounced, slow your step down to an edging forward, gliding motion. The more cautious and deliberate the approach, the greater are the chances of success.

Some streams appear more prone to wading ripple than others, although it should relate solely to depth and current strengths. Certain rivers tumble noisily along, the water breaking and bubbling, tinkling and tearing, ripping and rushing as it courses downstream. Others, such as the Scandinavian streams, have a strange quality of surface tension which seems almost reluctant to break and they run eerie and silent, as though the viscous nature of the surface tried to avoid making any sound. Low atmospheric pressure can create a similar situation on the most friendly of streams. Just before a thunderstorm the light and barometric conditions combine to give the surface a slick, oily sheen.

Rocks and other solid bank materials do not transmit the vibrations of footsteps as readily as soil and boggy leaf-mould deposits. In areas where there are vast accumulations of dead trees and leaves bordering a river, fish are warned of the approach of an angler long before he has reached the banks of the stream.

I have had the opportunity to fish crystal-clear chalk streams, where the most stealthy approach has been frustrated by the first motion of the cast. The initial rod movement — in the daylight — causes the fish to dart for the sanctuary of the weeds. Yet the same place at dusk, fished with care, gives the ego a boost, as the fish rise freely to the feathered offering. Waders are used only to position the angler in places that allow a clear backcast and help keep a low profile by kneeling in the shallow runs.

I have one rather interesting story to relate which occurred while wading (other than irrelevant tales which concern quite commonplace and ignominious wettings), on a salmon outing.

The location was the classic salmon lie, a gravel bed on which I stood in water up to my knees, the stones sloping down to a rock ledge that I would speculate was six or seven-feet deep, and a solid wall of rock facing me. For such shallow water the current was surprisingly strong, and the pebbles lifted between my feet and clattered against the legs of the black rubber hip boots that I wore. The waders, I recall, were a purchase I had saved hard for. They had a hole from a particularly vicious thorn branch acquired on my first visit to the stream, which I had repaired with a bright red cycle patch.

As I cast the fly across the stream and allowed it to swing across the flow, the sunshine showed up the complete gravel bed, disappearing into smoky green depths of the rock shelves; the fly stood out clearly in the water. It was a pleasant spot to fish and I repeated the cast with an almost automatic irreverence. While observing the surroundings and the river in general, a movement caught my eye. A trout, about sixteen-inches long left the darkness of the pool, and swam determinedly up the far edge of the main stream to a position opposite me. Then, it suddenly darted, shark-like, directly across the river at top speed and crashed into my leg; ricocheted upstream from the impact, turned, dashed back to the far side of the stream, and sped back to the depths of the pool.

To this day I am quite at a loss to explain the behavior of this fish, unless it was the unique challenge of the small red patch on the ankle of my black hip waders stirring up the gravel, that triggered off the attack by the ill-tempered piscine bruiser. It is sufficient to say that this is the only occasion that I have encountered a fish that has adopted such an aggressive attitude towards me!

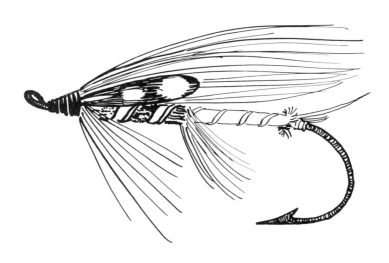

CHAPTER 10

The Importance of Correct Rod Manipulation

It is the mastery of fly manipulation that governs the success of the fisherman after he has reached a level of casting proficiency which allows positive tackle control and line placement. When he is armed with the knowledge that fish, when surface feeding, look through a cone-shaped window, that refraction and light pattern play an important role when the offering of the angler is detected and the stimulated rise occurs, when he is aware that under the water the reverse surface-mirror condition enables the fish to observe the fly movements (the underside of the lure from below and, in the reflection above, the upper portions), he is well beyond the tyro stage.

Under these circumstances, it cannot be sufficiently emphasized that the rod can be made to transmit and inject a large amount of action (life) to the fly that is impossible to achieve by solely using hand retrieve motions, incorporated into the recovery patterns of the line.

A story to substantiate this statement came about while I was boat fishing with a friend for bass. We were casting into a sloping, rock-shelved shore line that bass tend to favor, using hair-winged streamer flies, (mine a silver, red, and yellow combination — a Mickey Finn, my companion's a white and red creation — a Parma Belle) and, while I was enjoying considerable success, he had not had a single take. To save changing flies, I passed him my outfit to use and I took over his tackle. With my first two casts I hooked and released two small fish, but my partner had not had a single strike. We analyzed the situation. Our first thoughts had been that the red and yellow streamer had been the reason for my success which had now to be re-evaluated. I watched closely as he cast faultlessly to the rocky shore line, paused to allow the fly to sink, and then started the short stabbing retrieve which I had employed to get action. I suddenly diagnosed the fault. Whereas I had gently vibrated the rod tip as I stripped back line, he was recovering the line in the same manner, but did not move the rod. This may seem to be a very minor point at first appraisal, yet it is very often the difference between a good day's work and a fishless outing.

The rod can supply a fantastic amount of life to the feathered offering when the rod tip is rocked: to prove it, place the fly into the water and first strip back the fly by pulling the line through the guides and watch what is a rather wooden result. Now strip back in exactly the same manner, while gently shaking the rod and observe the amazing difference. The feathers from which it is made will be seen to pulsate in a most attractive way, the rod movement transforming the fly from simply a hook with silk, fur, and feathers, to the semblance of an alive, swimming creature.

A story I heard told by Jack Sutton, a great Canadian angler, relates to the other end of the scale as far as fly movement is concerned and I tell it to lend significance to the fact that there is no sure-fire technique for catching fish with a fly and that success generally follows the angler with the most skill, the greatest knowledge, and the largest variety of methods.

Jack, as he told it, had not enjoyed a particularly fruitful morning's fishing and had stopped to have a sandwich and a cup of coffee. As this was in the days of gut leaders, he had put the rod down at his feet and had left the line and fly in the water to keep the leader wet (the gut leader was liable to break if allowed to get dry and brittle). The fly had sunk to the bottom of the stream and, as he looked around, his foot knocked the rod — and instantly the tip whipped down as a fish took the fly! The fish was quickly landed, and the rod placed in the same position: a bite of food, another drink of coffee, a tap of the rod with the foot — another fish on! (It is now that I must warn the reader of Jack's sense of humor). This happened again and again, until he had emptied the thermos and eaten all his food after which, he claimed, his luck ended. Jack would round off his story, with a twinkle in his eye, by saying that if he had had more sandwiches and coffee he would have emptied the river of fish.

What Jack Sutton discovered back in the 1920's — and I fondly like to think he was the first — was to receive great acclaim in Europe forty years later. That is, that fish will actually pick up a fly from the bed of a stream or lake, and even pluck a fly from a weed, on the assumption that it is an aquatic creature. It means that the really patient nymph fisherman can occasionally outfish conventional fly casters by using a painfully slow skip-and-wait method of line recovery.

CHAPTER 11

The Fly

A SHORT HISTORY

The basic fly used by the angler has progressed a long way since that first offering made from red wool and two feathers described by Aelian, yet today's flies still retain a definite physical resemblance. They wear only a more sophisticated garb and are better attired for the work.

Hooks too have advanced from those times, although still perfectly recognizable. Even in the Waltonian era they were individually made from needles, and the *Book of St. Albans* contains instructions on how to make and temper the metal for a hook and raise the barb, which is explained with a beautiful simplicity based on the color tones of heated metal. Eyed hooks in the form that we know them today did not arrive on the angling scene until the late eighteen, early nineteen-hundreds and, though there were hooks with flattened ends and needle eyes long before this period, the lack of any material suitable to knot onto them would possibly halt investigation and any experimentation in this direction. A tapered shank was the most satisfactory method of attaching a length of brittle hair with a binding of silk thread to the hook, and the fly on top of the binding proved the best utilization of available materials at that time.

The story of the history of the hook industry, which had its birth in England, is rather interesting. During the period of the Black Plague (terminated by the Great Fire of London), the wealthy needle-making families moved their craft to the small town of Redditch in Worcestershire, away from the troubles of London. Needle making and fishhook manufacture being similar pursuits, Redditch became for a long while the hook-making center of the world. Today, however, Norway, Japan, France, and the U.S. are placed above Britain in the production of fish hooks, although the famous Partridge Hooks from Redditch are still held in high regard.

The period during Izaak Walton's lifetime was a time troubled by upheaval and strife. The Black Plague in London was in the final stage of entrenchment after three centuries of devastation in Europe, having claimed more than half the total population during that time. The plague was carried by black rats. In Britain the disease was concentrated in the place where the rats found the most suitable habitat — the city of London. The city had grown around the settlement made by the Romans — tightly packed narrow streets, thatched roofs, and a crowded populace living in an environment that suffered from a tragically inadequate waste disposal and an almost non-existent sewerage system.

In the country districts, the indigenous brown rat had eliminated the immigrant black species, which arrived as stow-a-ways on vessels from the continent, and thrived in the Thames Riverport of London, to persist until the flames of the Great Fire of London conquered the plague and its cause in 1665.

Walton was in his sixties when this occurred. During his lifetime there had been continual political strife, with Charles the Second and Oliver Cromwell fighting for control of the country (the Cavaliers and Roundheads religious clashes), and life must have been very difficult. Consider these aspects when you read the writings of Walton and Cotton, and in their lyrical words find concealed both a mental escape and a means of physical relaxation in the art of angling at a time when history was far from the easy-going life that one is likely to believe was the pattern of living during the Waltonian period. I feel sure that this is one of the main reasons for the accolades showered on Walton by his contemporaries, admittedly written only for those who had enjoyed the luxury of an education and could read! The *Book of St. Albans* was originally a reference for the nobility. It is we who follow that reap the true benefit from their work.

Walton not only wrote a book which laid out a method of angling procedures but offered a therapeutic pursuit for the soul. The words of Izaak Walton and Edward Grey hold the same message at the present time as they did when they were first penned.

The fly that Aelian first spoke of, the twelve that are described in the *Book of St. Albans,* and the list of sixty that Charles Cotton detailed in *The Compleat Angler,* established the form of the feathered offering.

In the beginning, flies were obviously made to appear similar to those seen on the water and being taken by the fish. The fact that they sank was of little consequence when the offering was accepted, which I surmise led the old-time fly fishermen to assume that it was taken as a sunken or drowned representation of the insects seen flying over the water. As time progressed, more and more patterns of flies were added to the list of fur and feather creations, some bearing no resemblance to any living creature, yet with the ability to take fish. Luckily however, the popularity of a fishing fly is based solely upon performance rather than appearance, a situation which tends to keep the area of fly patterns under control and there are mammoth lists of fly dressings which are now a part of the history of fly fishing that pay homage only to the productivity of the fly-tying fishermen of the past.

It was not until the middle of the 1800's that a closer look was taken at the fly being used to tempt fish. Some thought was then given to what the majority of the skillfully tied and beautifully created offerings of silk, fur, and feathers were actually supposed to be!

From the first studies of entomology, it was apparent that the sunk fly generally simulated nymphs, larvae or pupae of water-dwelling insects. It has taken almost a full century for fly fishermen to accept the situation and, almost grudgingly, discard some of the traditional patterns and conventional dressings for the more innovational styles of modern fly-fishing creations.

A knowledge of entomology is very useful to the fly fisherman, for it assists greatly in the identification of the floating insect, or underwater creature and helps in the selection of the right fly for a particular place at a certain time. Yet the ritual of changing flies until a pattern is accepted is still the standard procedure. This could be a psychological reaction on the part of the fly fisherman, based on the fact that Latin nomenclature is used for the creatures classified by entomological study, which has contri-

The Anatomy of a Fly

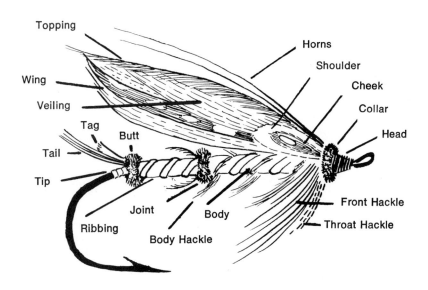

Topping

Horns

Shoulder

Wing

Cheek

Veiling

Collar

Tag

Head

Butt

Tail

Tip

Front Hackle

Joint

Throat Hackle

Body

Ribbing

Body Hackle

buted to the abhorrence of change from ancient to modern, plus perhaps a sentimental subconscious loyalty to the conventional fly, ingrained in the intellect of generations of fly fishermen after so many centuries of service.

Change is not advocated for its own sake — the illustrious patterns, the names of which have such a magical ring and so noble a history: Black Gnat, Greenwell's Glory, Cahill, Green Drake, Brown Hackle, are not to be cast aside but rather supplemented with more suggestive dressings, based on the knowledge gained from the study of entomology. The dry-fly fishermen of the English chalk streams were the first anglers to use the information provided by entomological investigation at the turn of the century and works on the subject up to the present time by men such as Halford, Mosely, C. F. Walker, Harris, and Goddard in Britain, and Rhead, Jennings, Wetzel, Flick, and Schwiebert in North America, provide the angler, be he a wet-fly expert or dry-fly specialist, with an enormous amount of valuable information that is only now being fully utilized.

Fly fishermen, on the whole, are a strange breed. A new development in rod design and manufacturing technique is received with acclaim; a better leader material is hailed with enthusiasm; a superior line is adopted immediately; a product introduced that offers advantages over the old is accepted without question; yet to suggest that some of the flies stored in aluminium boxes and leather wallets are double counterfeits (fraudulent to both angler and fish) is paramount to blasphemy, to be viewed with a mixture of disdain, suspicion, and disregard! It can perhaps be explained by the simple fact that an offering which does not resemble the appearance of the traditional fly has a hard time inspiring the confidence of the fisherman.

Fly fishing, until the latter part of the nineteenth century, was a system of fishing flies in and below the surface of the stream (a method which today would be classified as the standard wet-fly technique). However, in the Winchester area of southern England, the sport was a recreational pastime for the schoolboys on the Itchen, a river famous for its trout which are partial to feeding on floating insects. Here a truly momentous angling event occured. It was discerned that a fly unwetted by casting would on the first delivery float upon the surface and be accepted more readily by the fish. With this discovery, the sport was split into two emphatic divisions. Suddenly flies were being tied to "float," (no one knows by whom or where, save that it was rooted in that area) and it was here that the development of the upstream cast evolved.

Entomology has not only guided more factually the shape, shade, and size of the dry fly, it has explained the metamorphosis stream insects undergo, (nymph, dun, spinner, and spent). It has discovered motional mannerisms peculiar to specific groups of insects that can be reproduced by subtle rod movements. The wet-fly fisherman found that entomology disclosed what his sunk offering actually imitated and, more importantly, told him how the underwater creatures moved, what actions they produced prior to hatching, and the behavioral pattern they adopted when emerging.

A new breed of fly fisherman is presently involved in the sport. Anglers are taking a refreshingly new approach to the whole scene of fly fishing, and are listening to experts who advocate the commonsense fly-fishing knowledge that entomology lends to the sport — what the fly is supposed to represent; when it may be best employed; where it can be used; how it should be fished.

Let me emphasize that what I have said is not intended to be the death knell for the traditional fly. It has been written in the hope that more fly fishermen will give some thought to what is ultimately the most important piece of their tackle — the fly.

CHOOSING THE FLY

An understanding of the subaqueous life upon which fish feed is a great help to the modern angler. With each new season fishing becomes more demanding, due to increasing angling pressure (which means fewer fish per angler), and it is natural that the anglers with the greatest skill and acumen take the largest numbers of fish.

Within its liquid environment the fish has a broad range of food items from which to choose, both below the surface and upon it. The angler has to decide which food type he wishes to simulate with his fly (somewhat governed by the method he uses to fish it), or to bring attention to it by his style of angling. Some flies are intended to be suggestive of a natural food form and deceive, while others are purely attractors and provoke attack either from curiosity or anger, and are fished accordingly. Occasions are sometimes encountered when the most clumsy presentation will be taken unhesitatingly and any pattern accepted with equal enthusiasm, while at other times (alas more prevalent) when the situation is reversed, and the most correct and precise offering will be treated with disdain. Such is the challenge of fly fishing.

The subaqueous creatures, some of which live only part of their existence under water and have a life cycle that lifts them above the surface, provide fish with their major food source, both below and above the water. A fly fisherman should have some knowledge of the subject in order to analyze the particular situations he encounters while fishing.

Here is a general description of life cycle of a subaqueous creature: from egg to nymph or larva; then in some cases to pupa; then to the emerged insect, the Dun, or subimago; after which, in some cases, a molt to the Spinner, or imago (the egg-laying stage); and, finally, the Spent fly (a drowned or dying insect).

The main insect orders that are found in most bodies of fresh water are:

ephemeroptera	mayflies
trichoptera	caddis flies
diptera	midges, gnats, crane flies
plecoptera	stone flies
odonata	dragon and damsel flies
megaloptera	fish flies and dobson flies (hellgrammites)

Using tinsel for the ribbing of a fly, gives it a certain degree of flash (and helps make the body more secure), but is not there solely for appearance's sake — although it may have been, originally. It actually imitates a tiny reservoir of air that nymphs carry within the subaqueous jacket they wear. A fly, freshly caught in the current, trapped by the stream, and drawn under by the flow, has a sheen of air clinging to its tiny appendages when it first sinks. Here is another useful role played by a ribbing material, bound tightly over a fibrous body material such as fur or wool — it has the ability to hold minute pockets of air trapped amongst the filaments from which the body is made.

Heavy, down eye hooks are used for wet flies, and lightweight, up-eyed irons for dry. Stiff cock hackles, buoyant body materials with not too many tail fibers (otherwise a capillary effect is created which sinks the fly), and wings that possess the suggestion of movement within the shimmering light pattern are used for the floating offering. For the sunk fly, soft hen hackles and other absorbent substances that will soak up the water, sink quickly, and react to the play of the current, are used.

Long shanked lure hooks, for attractor patterns with all types of hackles, hair, feather, and fiber of every hue are used for wing materials. Bodies are made from all manner of things to create a fish-attracting, strike-provoking combination of color and form.

Two particular aspects connected with the fishing of a fly have long fascinated me and, where the capricious nature of the feeding habits of the fly fisher's quarry is concerned, may be worth pursuing: taste and smell.

A fly fisherman can learn from other branches of the sport. Carp seem to be partial to dough balls, boiled potatoes, and floating bread crust; rainbow trout are taken with marshmallows and cheese. It is common practice for British sea trout anglers to impale two or three maggots (gentles) on the hooks of flies used for fishing at dusk to make the offering more attractive and delay the ejection of the fly. Could there be a taste factor involved here?

I recollect from my earliest fishing days, as a nine year old, using natural minnows for bait, which during May and June were readily accepted. In early July, a salted minnow was preferred over the natural, and by the end of the month, only the soft belly area was torn from the bait without any contact being made with the hook. By August the fish showed no interest in the bait at all.

Food Forms that Are Imitated by the Angler with a Fly

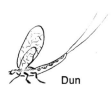 Dun

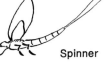 Spinner

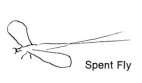 Spent Fly

Stone Fly

Fish Fly

 Caddis

Caddis Larva

Midge Pupa

Caddis Pupa

Freshwater Shrimp

Mayfly Nymphs:
Gills on Abdomen

Stone Fly Nymphs:
Gills on Thorax

The Role of Suggestion Rather than Exact Imitation

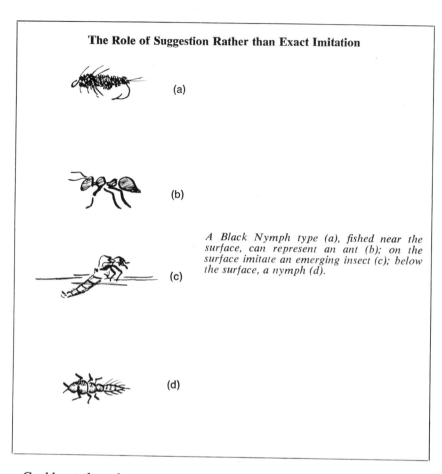

(a)

(b)

(c)

(d)

A Black Nymph type (a), fished near the surface, can represent an ant (b); on the surface imitate an emerging insect (c); below the surface, a nymph (d).

Could not the subaqueous food forms, within the natural cycle, not only reach a maximum nutritional point, but also achieve a peak of flavor . . . . munchy mayflies, sweet young minnows, crunchy caddis larva, nutty stone fly nymphs, palatable spinners with the tell-tale yellow egg sack, scrumptious midges? I do not mean this to be taken as simply a frivolous comment nor, on the other hand, taken too seriously either. It is purely food for thought. The taste factor could explain the occasional frustrating selectivity of fish, rejecting one food form in preference to another.

Jack Sutton, a superb fly tier, used only untreated feathers that still had the natural oils on them, claiming that the scent of the natural hackles improved the fishing qualities of his creations. Today his flies are collectors' items among Canadian fly fishermen, so beautifully were they tied.

A fish can take a fly for various reasons — as a food form, as an explora-tory bite, or as a savage reaction to some alien intruder. There is no magic formula for a fly dressing, no sure-fire pattern that guarantees success, no method that will absolutely take fish.

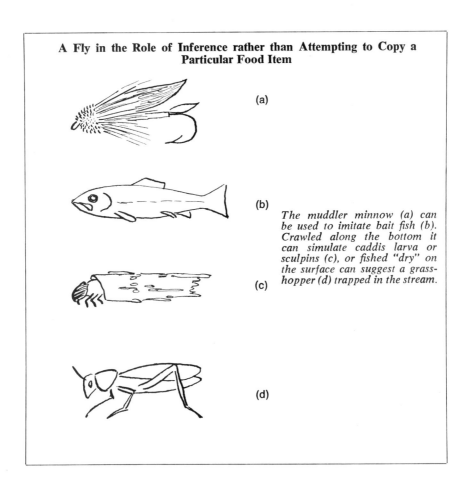

A Fly in the Role of Inference rather than Attempting to Copy a Particular Food Item

(a)

(b)

The muddler minnow (a) can be used to imitate bait fish (b). Crawled along the bottom it can simulate caddis larva or sculpins (c), or fished "dry" on the surface can suggest a grass-hopper (d) trapped in the stream.

(c)

(d)

FLY FISHING WITH STREAMERS, BUCKTAILS, AND SIMILAR LURES

The number of feather and hair-dressed hooks which can be categorized as fly-fishing lures is substantial, and there will be no attempt to classify them specifically other than to separate them into two main groups: flies that vaguely suggest food forms (bait fish and other subaqueous creatures) and those that are purely attractor patterns, a presumption which even then is difficult, as the method of fishing is more often than not the deciding factor.

Today the name "streamer fly" embraces all flies which fit into the lure and bait-fish imitation category and, without doubt, no fly type has done more to expand the versatility and enlarge the domain of the fly-rod fisherman than the streamer.

It is perhaps safe to assume that this type of fly was first tied to represent small bait fishes. However, during the evolution of the fly style and the development of the method of fishing with it, there was a quick departure from the original concept, when color combinations with no counterparts in nature were found to work even better than a form which attempted to mimic a living creature.

This type of fly is normally dressed on a long shank hook (although there are variations, using two and three standard-length hooks, tied one behind the other) to provide a suitable area on which to tie a body and roughly simulate the form of the creature it is intended to imitate. The size of the offering allows a more imaginative approach to be used by the fly tier as it provides greater scope to the range of materials which can be employed in making them. Over the years a multitude of innovative creations have appeared from the work benches of the fly dressers that for a time had the characteristics of their places of origin: the hackle types of Europe (Terrors), the hair-wing patterns which were essentially North American (Bucktails), and the feather styles developed in New Zealand (Matuka).

The materials from which the lure is created contribute much to the performance that can be extracted from the offering — in respect to the texture rather than the color. Hair is normally a stiff, resilient winging material ideal for a fly that is to be fished in flowing water and, where the angler by employing the wet-fly technique, can produce a living motion, swimming, "kick" from the lure by the teasing action of rod movement. The pull of the current compresses the fibers around the hook and, when it is allowed to drift, the resilient hair springs back to the position the wing originally held. Skillful rod manipulation can produce a pulsating action from the offering as it moves in the flow and this attractive action, combined with the color and flash that is built into the creation, are the elements which induce an investigatory, hungry, or savage strike at the lure from the piscine quarry. All materials used in the construction of the wings of feather and hair-fly lures can produce to some degree the suggestion of attraction, bunches of hackles, synthetic fibers, strips of feather, bucktail, and all types of hair. Bodies are created from an even broader assortment of materials — silk, wool, fur, synthetics, herl, and tinsels. There are unending aspects of color, shape, density of shade, combinations of material and tone, flash, translucency, and size that are intended to stimulate a feeding impulse, arouse curiosity, or provoke an attack.

To a certain extent the materials from which the fly is made are a guide to the fisherman as to how it will fish best; soft feathers, fur, and hen hackles will work best in slow water, while firm hair, stiff fur, and cock hackles are better in faster current. Once the fisherman is aware of the potential and capability of a fly type, he can fish it accordingly and, furthermore, when the fisherman advances to this stage of expertise he enlarges his repertoire of angling technique: the same fly, for example, can be fished through a section of holding water first as a lamed bait fish with only a slight amount of motion imparted by the rod (to hopefully promote a curiosity acceptance); secondly as a wounded minnow (to perhaps spark off a feeding impulse) producing a quiver and a darting and drifting action with the rod, and finally (to possibly cause a territorial demonstration of dominance), a purely attractor method of presentation — with a twitch, pull, twitch, pull, pull, pause, of rod manipulation — to create interest.

The design of any lure should be built around the knowledge that a fish, when it strikes at the feathered lure, hits at the fly rather like a dog takes a bone; seizing it sideways or, it moves on to it from the rear. Thus the gape and barb of the hook should be at the rear of the lure, without too much overhang of winging material to ensure that contact is made when the line is drawn taut. Attention must also be given to the position of the wing (the setting of the rake of angle — high for fast water, low for slow to obtain maximum action) to ensure that the materials do not wrap under the body and entwine around the bend of the hook (over-long hackles are often guilty of this fault) which eliminate the emission of living motion.

The two and more stripes of color provided by the wing construction and body tone of the fly are an attractive profile feature of the long shanked lure. The action that the greater bulk of materials produce when drawn through the water and the action's larger visual image contribute greatly to the success of fly type.

The fly lure fished at any stream depth can produce a strike. The modern sinking line added a new dimension to fishing by allowing the fly to be fished close to and on the stream bed. There are numerous types of bait fish which hide amongst the stones and weeds at lower depths and a fly lure, hopped and jumped across the river bottom, will take fish when drifted styles of fly fishing will not produce.

Generalized Anatomy of a Fish

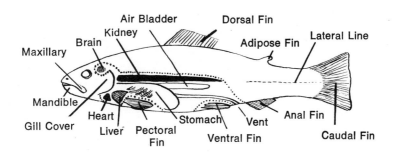

During the course of any season most of the larger fish of any species succumb to the fatal attraction of the fly lure, and the reason for the situation is not difficult to fathom. The larger fish are more inclined to feed on food in keeping with their proportions and nature, within the pyramid of liquid-dwelling life forms, including a predatory system whereby the large live upon the small. There is an instinctive mechanism whereby piscine feeding action is ruled by the factor of energy expended being placed against nutriment gained, which explains why most of the mature fish are taken on large flies. However, when there is an abundance of smaller food forms, the larger fish will feed quite readily, all things finally being dependent on the urgency of the feeding stimulus.

CHAPTER 12

How to Read Water
and Find Fish

The skill to read the water, allied with adroit handling of tackle are the two keys to successful stream fishing. The angler must have an understanding of the habitat of his piscine quarry, as well as a comprehension of the mobile liquid element in which it dwells.

A dry-fly fisherman must assess the surface current, its speed, and subleties of flow. He must cast his line to assist the drift of his fly and avoid the tricks of the current from making a mockery of his presentation. The wet-fly angler must observe the surface movement of the stream and relate the picture of the flow to what lies below. In the discussion on the basic method of wet-fly fishing, the aspect of efficient current penetration is emphasized and in fast-flowing water the use of a short leader in combination with a sinking or sinking tip line is recommended to obtain the best results.

A knowledge of the speed layers contained within the sectional profile of the water flow is invaluable to the sunk-fly fisherman. The awareness that fish look for food in places where the current is less fierce (where edible morsels are brought to them rather than having to forage for them) and familiarity with the fact that fish choose to dwell in spots which offer shelter and protection, provide the angler with a tremendous advantage over his adversary. Some fly fishermen possess the talent to look at a section of water and almost instinctively locate the areas that hold fish.

Surface signs are not solely the concern of the dry-fly angler; the visible turbulence is a condition created by the configuration of the river bed, and it is the sub-surface flow speed which is the concern of the wet-fly fisherman. Armed with the quite rudimentary information that follows, the ability to read the stream will be within the grasp of any angler.

The experienced angler will invariably make an appraisal of the river before commencing to fish: studying the stream, watching for activity — feeding fish or hatching flies, and almost subconsciously observing the main core of the current, making mental notes of the best stations from which to present the fly to which particular spots. The deepest part of the moving water course containing the wandering body of the stream as it flows along is the *thalweg,* an old German word used in the terminology of modern stream management. It describes the section of the stream that possesses the major motional flow of water. It is usual for the denizens of the stream to be located in, or along, the two edges of the *thalweg,* carving first one bank then cutting into the other, as its channel meanders from side to side down the course of the river bed.

Fish that are susceptible to the allure of the feathered offering of the fly fisherman are predators by nature. Stretches of the stream that are devoid of the species being angled for because of shallow water and lack of protective cover by day, will, as the light fades, receive marauding visits from fish that remain hidden during the daylight hours. It is surprising the number of large fish that are caught out of position and taken from the most unlikely spots at dusk by fly fishermen who are aware of this fact.

I remember my first experience with this kind of angling knowhow many years ago. I was fishing for trout on a small stream near the Scottish border. As night approached, I hurried back downstream to reach the road before dark (parents seem to worry unduly about the solitary angling activities of a twelve-year old). It was a soft balmy, early June evening and I crossed an ankle-deep, shallow run in order to shorten the distance I had to travel.

There was a sudden explosion of watery activity as I stepped into the stream, as startled fish sped back to the pool below in a frenzy of splashing haste, which erased all thoughts of heading homeward.

In those days it was standard procedure to fish with three flies on the leader and I remember quite clearly the Northern patterns I was using. A Coachman on the point (always, as now, a good fly at dusk), above it a Partridge and Orange, and on the top dropper, a Woodcock and Yellow, both dropper flies being spider types, hackled without wings.

I knew the stream well. Indeed, if my academic knowledge had been equal to my familiarity of the angling venue, my parents would have been much happier. I headed downstream to the next shallow riffle similar to the one I had just discovered, crammed with foraging fish. With my first cast, made in the rapidly fading light, the Coachman took a fish, and its wild battle, fought in such thin water alarmed the other fish but made a spectacular sight as panicking trout slashed and turned and arrowed downstream.

Elated with my discovery, I made straight for the next shallow run and with the initial cast had a double! The point and the middle flies accounted for the pair, accompanied by the same splashing downstream rush from the rest of the startled fish feeding in the ankle-deep water.

My triumphant twilight escapade continued, with another trout being taken at the next riffle. Now, almost casting blind at the next spot, I had a take on each fly for, almost simultaneously, there were three decisive strikes transmitted through the rod, coinciding with the immediate flurry of activity as the fish evacuated the shallow water. At the same instant my

142

leader broke at the loop! It was an educational and quite a unique experience, the like of which I have never met with again. However, the knowledge gained from it has helped me catch fish in places at dusk that other fishermen would never think to try.

The disclosure of the fact that shallow moving water can provide a bonanza of sport for the sunk-fly fisherman at dusk, does not mean that the stiller stretches of the stream should not receive similar attention as darkness approaches. It is in these slower-flowing areas, a foot or so in depth where shoals of bait fish safely congregate in the daytime, that the biggest fish are taken on fly at night, for it is in such places that the larger fish find an abundant food supply.

An upstream approach, using any of the forms of fly fishing, places the fisherman below his quarry, which is the most concealed area from which to cast. At first glance it would appear to be the natural direction from which to advance, the rear being the blind spot of a fish facing upstream. There are, however, the signals of alarm to consider; smaller fish moving ahead of the progress of the angler; ripple warning; and, unless the cast is made at an angle, the line and leader will cover the fish before the fly — a situation that will normally frighten mature fish immediately.

Using the downstream method, the same alerting elements must be given consideration, including the extra disadvantage of the fact that the fish may get the benefit of visual detection. There is the chance that mud may be stirred up and give advance notice of the approaching angler. However, by going with the stream flow, making use of available cover, and by slow stealthy progress, the fly is the first part of the tackle presented to the fish.

The skillful use of the equipment — the accurate and delicate placement of the line and adroit manipulation of the fly play a strategic role in successful stream fishing. Casts will be made from a crouched or kneeling position a great deal of the time and, occasionally, executed backhand on the lateral travel path across the body. Indeed, there are times when the overhead style can rarely be used because of trees and high banks and the line for the major part of the time will be cast on planes that parallel the water. It is on such stretches as these that the roll cast fulfills a useful service.

The mechanics of the cast are constant, regardless of the plane upon which it is executed. This principle applies to both styles of casting — aerialized or upon the water. There may be an occasional spot where the fly fisherman will have to control the line below the level on which he stands. This may have to be done where the bank is high and the stream either too deep or unsuitable to wade, with perhaps trees forming an arch above the section of water to be reached, or when a cast must be thrown under a bridge.

I recall one such place that demanded this style of cast in order to place the fly in a piece of water that was created after a road had been made, leaving two lakes connected by a forty-yard length of concrete tunnel, eight-

feet wide and four-feet high. Shoals of small fish collected around the entrances of the tunnel, which usually contained a foot or so of slowly running water. The larger fish were in the habit of feeding on the easy meal provided by the bait fish, and then resting in the cool darkness of the tunnel, digesting their food in comfort and safety.

The openings at either side, cutting away from each lake, were built with rough stones sloping upward past the height of the tunnel to a point almost level with the road. By taking up a position to the side about eight feet from the opening and by gradually extending the line — below ground level — so that the false casts actually passed into the tunnel and then out over the lake, and by shooting extra line at release, it was possible to throw forty feet of line into the tunnel and take the occasional fish by casting underhand to a spot that most anglers would resignedly designate as an unfishable sanctuary.

During daylight fish will normally be found along the edges of the main flow of the stream, stationed in the secondary currents where the force of the water is less strong. They invariably adopt positions which afford both cover from predators and shelter from the current, in places which offer a good field of observation, and have a ready source of food drifted to them. However, the largest and more cautious of the species, during the summer months particularly when the water is low and clear, will remain hidden during the hours of daylight and will feed only under the cover of darkness, moving away from their chosen lair to forage the shallow areas of the stream where food is abundant.

Armed with this knowledge, the fly fisherman is able to take full advantage of the angling potential of the stream, and take fish from places that the less educated fisherman would ignore.

In order to keep as low as possible on the bank, Jim Hardy casts from a kneeling position. Note the slight but effective haul motion being incorporated into the casting action by a tiny wrist movement of the secondary hand to obtain greater line speed, which, in turn, gives the angler superior line control.

CHAPTER 13

The Wet Fly

FISHING THE WET FLY IN MOVING WATER

When using the wet fly, the angler searches for fish willing to accept it. With the dry fly he stalks a feeding fish. This description is perhaps an over-simplification of the two basic styles of fly fishing. However, it is a good starting point.

The submerged piscine offering of the fly fisherman, the wet fly, fished in moving water, is a technique that uses the flow of the current to assist the presentation of the fly. The line is cast at an angle across the stream and, being held anchored at the rod tip, swings back to the bank from which the line was thrown, allowing the fly to cover a circular band of the stream. This is possibly the nearest method of fly fishing as we know it today to that which was practised in Walton's day.

Casts are normally made at a forty-five degree angle, and the rod is generally rocked to transmit an element of life to the fly as it swings to a point below the angler. When it reaches the stage of the angled downstream journey where line, leader, and fly hang in the current, the line is fished back a few feet in short, jabbing retrieve motions before being cast out again. This action is made in the event that the fly has been followed by an interested fish.

The action used by the angler, through the medium of the rod to produce a life-like motion in the fly and transmit a degree of attractiveness to the offering, can vary from a gentle vibration of the rod tip to simulate a struggling, helpless motion to a vigorous, darting swimming movement made by a quite positive shaking of the rod. The oscillations from the rod are transferred to the taut line, which results in the fly being affected to a similar (but lesser, because of the water) extent, and the materials from which the fly is constructed react alternately — first to the drawing of the line by the rod, an instant of drift, and then the pull of the current.

For wet-fly fishing with a sinking line in moving water, the leader need

146

not be longer than nine feet and in fast water five to six feet will give better angling results. When a floating line is employed for the downstream wet-fly, seven to nine feet prove adequate (of course with this buoyant line there is little chance of successfully probing the lower levels of water with the fly).

The angling procedure for downstream wet-fly fishing takes two forms. On large rivers, a constant length of line can be used and, after each cast made either from the bank or wading, a downstream pace is taken by the angler, who, by using this method, meticulously covers every section of water contained within his casting arc as he slowly progresses down the river. This is the method used on large rivers, and is the style adopted by American steelhead fishermen and trout fishermen on the Tweed, Tyne, or Tay in Britain.

On smaller rivers, a different procedure is used. The fisherman, using the same basic wet-fly fishing technique, on finding a suitable spot, will take up a position that leaves the desired piece of water to be fished within comfortable casting distance and, by gradually extending his line after each cast by ten or fifteen inches, will cover within his casting arc all the available water. When the stretch has been thoroughly searched, the line is recovered and the angler moves on to another suitable spot.

Fishing the wet fly on tiny streams, be it the creeks and feeders of North America or the brooks, becks, and burns of Europe, provides a special challenge. A later section dealing with fishing small waters and embracing the facets of fly fishing them, will deal with the subject in more detail.

It is said that in moving water fish find the bulk of their food in the upper and lower levels of the current, with the middle section of flow an area of little activity due to the fact that it carries little sustenance. Very possibly, this is true.

Taking a sectional view of stream flow, it will be discovered that the pace of motion in the volume of water movement is slower at the river bed than it is in the upper regions, because of the frictional contact of the moving liquid mass against the sides and bottom of the stream. The riffles, broken water, and slicks that are visible on the surface denote signs of turbulence which are caused by the contact the water has with the stream bed and, the rougher the river bottom, the greater the frictional effect becomes. Even what appears to be smoothly flowing water has slower contact areas. Indeed, where there are boulders and cut-out rock shelves, the moving liquid mass far from being a constant current flow, uniform from top to bottom, is cushioned, lifted, pushed, and diverted, leaving sections contained within the moving water mass that are quite still. These are places where food items accumulate. These are the spots where fish choose to position themselves without expending energy to fight the current.

Sectional View of Stream Flow

Current flow in relation to composition of the stream bed.

Intelligent use of this knowledge can greatly increase the angling results of the wet-fly fisherman. Over the years, the use of long tapered leaders has become fashionable and has developed into a habit among the fly-fishing fraternity. Their popularity is based on rumors that they lend better presentation to the fishing of the surface film nymph, spent insect imitations used in conjunction with a floating line, and other forms of dry-fly work. Some of these leaders are twelve to eighteen-feet long and, for the placement of floating and nymphal offerings, they perform an excellent function. However, the advantages of long leaders for surface fishing are completely erased in sunk line wet-fly technique.

The leader is so lacking in weight that the wet fly never penetrates the water flow to the depth achieved by the line, which means that the fly is never in a position to attract the attention of a fish, nor can it be placed in a deeper spot to be the cause of temptation.

From what has been discussed regarding sectional fluid pace, the reader can visualize a sinking line furnished with a long leader, placed in the stream. It will be observed that, although the line has knifed through the current flow, the leader is held higher in the current, while the fine tippet section is gripped in the major stream motion and the fly is held in the fastest section of the stream flow, unable to penetrate the moving liquid mass. At the end of the fishing cast the line is drawn fully taut, the line rises to the surface pulling with it the leader and the fly. The angler makes another cast, oblivious that his feathered offering has not been anywhere near the places where the fish actually are. A short leader is necessary for successful wet-fly fishing.

Presentation of the Fly in Fast Water

A.   *Sinking line with long leader.*
B.   *Fast sinking line with short leader.*

The recognized method of tackle handling and control for wet-fly fishing is to hold the rod low after the line has been cast to the selected spot at the desired angle. The line is trapped to the rod by the forefinger of the hand gripping the handle. As the line moves with the flow of the water, the rod is gently rocked to impart that extra tantalizing movement to the fly, and the tip is positioned to lead the line as it swings across the stream.

The rod should not point directly down the line, as a hard strike made at the fly would make the leader vulnerable to breakage, and the tippet section holding the fly could snap. By leading the line with the rod tip, there is always the resilient cushioning effect of the rod flex to absorb a strong take of the fly.

Intelligent use of initial line placement can vary the speed of fly presentation and the pace can be either slowed or increased, simply by the angle the line is placed on the water. An acutely-angled downstream cast will, in the arc of travel, present the fly at a slower speed than a cast made at the normal forty-five degree angle is capable of producing. A line thrown directly across the flow will swing the fly much faster than the normal delivery.

The take of the offering by the fish when using the wet fly in moving water is normally a self-hooking action (the line being taut to the rod) and when the solid underwater strike is detected the fish is firmly attached.

A knowledge of line placement in connection with presentational speed, and the awareness of the sectional stream flow and how it can be penetrated when combined with the art of fly motion, provide the wet-fly fisherman with a very effective angling method. The more expert exponents of this style of fishing claim that over the full angling season, taking all aspects of fly fishing into consideration, wet-fly fishing is the most productive.

UPSTREAM WET-FLY FISHING TECHNIQUES

The upstream wet fly is now almost completely the domain of the nymph fisherman and, although the type of offering may have changed, with the conventional fly discarded for the more innovational modern dressing, the basic method of angling remains very much the same.

A sunk fly, cast upstream and fished back with the current, is a style of angling that I encountered at an early age. For me it was a method devised to use while traveling back up-river after fishing the wet fly downstream. I recall quite clearly working out the problems that this technique involved; taking into account the fact that the fly could not be presented more slowly than the flow of the stream, and that the best type of offering from the meager range of flies that I then possessed was a spider dressing, such as a Brown Hackle, Black Spider, Gray Hackle, Partridge and Yellow, or Snipe and Purple. My favorite pattern was a fly with a purple wool body that had a sparse black hackle, with which I caught many fish. Any fly, really, which was tied with soft materials, one that would simulate a struggling insect in the turbulent water with fibers that would close instantly if pulled faster than the current, and open immediately when the stream flow and fly speed were constant; these were the main requirements. As well as the Black and Purple, I had another fly that I had tremendous faith in. It was a Red Tag with which I caught a good many grayling using the upstream casting method.

The upstream technique is at times very effective and all fly fishermen should have it in their repertoire. Fishing the upstream wet fly is a very demanding form of fly fishing, because the angler must keep in contact with the offering at all times in order to connect with an acceptance. This means that in particularly fast water the line must be stripped back in conjunction with the raising of the rod. This is the system adopted by most anglers to keep a reasonably taut line. The casts are angled ahead of the fisherman, who stands in the stream. In fast-flowing water, the circumstances make it folly to throw an over-long line (three to four rod lengths is ample). The technique requires that the rod be in a low position, close to the water when the delivery has been made. Immediately the line touches the stream under these conditions, the downstream drift occurs. The technique dictates that the secondary hand be employed to strip back the line in a single motion, recovered at the same pace as the current. When the secondary hand has moved to the full extent of travel (remember the line is controlled by the forefinger of the hand that grips the rod), to remain in contact with the fly, the rod is lifted slowly. The regained line in the secondary hand is best draped over the shoulder, rather than dropped in the water, and the hand quickly takes the line and draws the line back at the same rate as the stream — an action which, the more speedily it occurs, the more elevational

150

movement from the rod is held in reserve. When the stripping arm is once more at maximum extension, the rod again takes over the task of keeping contact with the fly, and is lifted still higher. At this point the leader loop should become visible above the water, and the cast is fished out by allowing the line to swing around and below the place where the angler stands before picking up the line and casting again, as fish occasionally follow the fly and invariably take it as it swings to the surface below the angler. Should a take occur at this stage of the cast, the tighten-on motion is done by the secondary hand tugging the line, as the full range of rod movement and arm extension have been utilized, keeping the line taut to the fly as it drifts downstream to the angler. Success depends on each hand performing a line-retrieving function in a manner which leaves either the rod hand or the stripping hand in a position of control, should a fish take the fly. This is the drill used by most anglers when fishing the fly upstream.

Watch the line where it enters the water while retrieving it and, should there be some change in the angle of entry or a slight alteration in speed or direction, tighten on, as the take can often be a very quiet, casual acceptance of the fly rather than a solid strike. With the upstream method of fishing there is little chance of working the fly by rod manipulation, as the tackle is usually being employed to the maximum to maintain a taut line to the offering, which makes the technique solely reliant on the natural presentation of the fly. The fly, in turn, must have an element of edibility to get results. In slower-flowing water the fly may be fished back in short hops. The important thing to remember is to have one hand free to make contact with a strike, for it is so easy to be caught in a situation where both hands are fully occupied with line-tending duties. One is then unable to answer the acceptance of the offering save with a muttered un-Waltonian word or two, as the fly is rejected.

In quick flowing, rock-strewn well-aerated, cascading, turbulent water where there are holes and deep pockets among half-exposed boulders, the upstream approach can provide some fast and often exciting fly fishing. Angling with a fly rod under such conditions dictates the use of a shorter length of line than was employed for the last described technique. Due to the speed of the current, two or three rod lengths is the maximum that can be controlled. There is a great deal of casting to be done! The procedure is: cast, finishing with a low rod position; aim to place the fly into the back-eddy spots behind the rocks; strip back the line with the secondary hand to maximum arm extension. Then lift the rod to keep in contact with the fly and, when the rod is held at almost the highest point possible, lift off with a flick of the wrist into the backcast. On the forward delivery, shoot the line that was recovered by the other hand, and repeat the process.

It is fast and furious fly fishing, requiring a great deal of concentration. When ten to fifteen casts are being made in a 60-second period, it is a style of fly fishing that soon lets one know how conditioned the casting arm is, and how much stamina one actually has!

The modern sinking-tip line is ideal for this style of fly fishing. When used in turbulent water among boulders, rock ledges, and water tumbles with churning bubble-filled back-currents, it has been responsible for taking above average-sized fish in bright sunshine. Well oxygenated spots are the favorite haunts of large fish in warm weather, especially when there is cover in the form of overhanging branches, undercut banks, or shelving rocks. Here is a point to remember, no matter how shallow the water appears to be.

It can be argued that a downstream approach could be equally effective. However, the cast made from below enables the angler to sink the fly, drift it into holding spots, guide it into backwaters, and keep in contact with the deceiving creation of fur and feather (which is presented in a more natural manner at a lower depth) all with a taut line. These presentational factors, together with superior tackle control — once the technique is fully mastered — are done more easily by an upstream approach and, of course, there is the advantage of concealment when the fly fisher casts from below.

With the faster methods of upstream fishing, governed by the speed of the water's flow, there is little chance of working the fly by rod manipulation, and the success of the technique is based solely on a natural and suggestive form of presentation. Fish, when taken by this method, have the hook solidly imbedded in the "scissors" part of the jaw (where the maxillary and mandible meet) and are rarely lost through a poor hold.

Upstream fly fishing combines two of the essential elements of angling with the fly: skillful presentation by the adroit handling of the equipment, and the use of a feathered offering that has the necessary qualities of deception. Fishing from below shows to the angler from another angle the complexities of the currents, swirl-backs and undertows, main and secondary flows, combined with the sectional speed-flow factor; all of which provide a very special challenge.

STRATEGIES FOR DOWNSTREAM NYMPH FISHING

The downstream technique of fishing with a sunk nymph is somewhat similar to the wet-fly method, although the imitative offering allows a more sophisticated approach (the subaqueous creatures the fly suggests) than is employed with the traditional wet fly, which is a mixture of simulation, stimulation, and aggravation. The nymphal creation is a deceiver rather than an attractor.

The similarity of the two styles ends, more or less, with the direction of the cast. The wet fly is used to combine the elements of attracting and deceiving and is fished in a purposeful, businesslike, thorough, searching manner. For sunk-fly fishing, with nymphs, the general angling approach is slower, the fly is employed solely to deceive, and the actual fishing is done in a style that simulates the natural movement of the underwater creature it is tied to represent. The two styles of fishing are sufficiently close, for the definition "flymphing" to be used to cover both methods. However, for instruction and information the styles have been dealt with individually.

A fish, once it has decided that an item may be palatable, is triggered into the first stage of a feeding or attack impulse. The second part of the stimulus consists of closer inspection and a quick sensory examination of the item (when it is taken into the mouth), leading to the final act which is either to devour the morsel or speedily eject it, if it is discovered to be contrary to what was expected.

There are quite elaborately dressed nymph types — some with plastic bodies, some with synthetic-fiber wing cases, and others with tiny rubber legs, that can occasionally be purchased in tackle stores. However, from experience, the more nondescript, ragged, and insignificant they appear, the better they do their work. This also applies to the conventional wet fly, for the more bedraggled the traditional flies become the better they take fish. Undoubtedly this upholds the theory of suggestion rather than an attempt at exact representation; inference rather than imitation.

Most commercially-tied flies are overladen with materials — and purposely so, for it is a well-known fact in the tackle trade that unless the flies look overdressed, the customer is reluctant to purchase them, even when superfluous materials must be removed to make the fly acceptable to the fish. A fly that will probably catch more fish right from the beginning, consisting of a pinch of drab, rough fur with just a hint of dull color, bound with a tiny piece of silver tinsel, and with a single turn of hackle attached to a hook, is not a saleable item! Strange are the ways of the angler!

Some of the subaqueous creatures that the nymph of the fly fisherman is meant to represent swim quite strongly. Others crawl, or dart quickly over short distances, or wriggle — facts which determine the method of fishing.

An important point for consideration is the size of the nymph. These small underwater denizens, during the stages of development that they undergo in the liquid element, grow from miniscule eggs to mature specimens. This, on reflection, infers that the size of the artificial being used need not necessarily be of a size relative to that which the creature attains when fully developed. Fish do not have intelligence in the accepted sense of the word, but they do have natural instinct, and it could be possible that an imitation of a mature insect, completely out of harmony with the rhythm of the food pattern of the stream, will arouse immediate suspicion. A good rule for the fly fisherman to follow is, when in doubt, use smaller sizes of nymph patterns.

The angling method, when using suggestive nymphs, is to cast across the flow (as was done for the wet-fly technique) and, as the line swings over the current, the tip of the rod — generally held higher than for wet-fly fishing — is used to transmit the various degrees of motion to the deceiving morsel of fur and feather. Some nymphs do not swim well, and in the current will be carried quite helplessly, while others that do have the ability to swim must struggle quite vigorously. It is these movements that the fly fisherman simulates as the line swings across the stream.

A method of nymph manipulation, developed by Jim Leisenring, is at times particularly deadly in slow moving water. The fly is allowed to swing with the current and sink; it is left a moment; then the rod is lifted, pulling the fly from the river bed to the surface (a technique that duplicates faithfully the action of an emerging nymph). The imitation, rising up through the water flow in the same manner as the natural, is an action that invariably attracts a fish inclined to feed, to strike greedily at an item of food it thinks is escaping. Should the water be deep, the secondary hand may also draw back line as the rod is raised to bring the fly to the surface. This action may be repeated if the fly is allowed to sink back to the bottom, and then pulled back to the top, for it mimics an action performed by some subaqueous creatures. The Leisenring Lift is a useful "flymph" fishing technique that can provide sport with a fly rod when underwater feeding activity has been observed.

A favorite method is to fish with the rod tip held at a point level with the eyes, for with the rod held at this height, by raising or lowering the angle of the rod, and by side movements, the fly can be maneuvered into areas the normal drift would miss, and the speed of the offering can be varied also, quickened by lifting, and slowed by a lowering of the rod.

When nymph fishing, the line in slower water is held less taut than when using the conventional fly patterns, yet the offering must still be presented on a reasonably tight leader and a straight line, otherwise there is a lack of contact between rod tip and fly. Take and rejection could occur without any transmission of the acceptance being sensed by the angler. A great many fishermen watch the progress of the line where it enters the water, and look for some small change in its speed of travel or a slight deviation of angle to detect a strike which, on some occasions (because of the natural presentation of the imitation), is so gentle that the take and the ejection of the fly is not noticed by the angler.

Weighted nymphs (hooks with fine lead or copper wire wrapped around the shank before the dressing is added) are not thought to be as effective as flies tied on stout hooks and when nymphal representations have to be fished deep, it is the line which performs the angling function best. The same applies in fast-water fishing, where the fly has to be fished close to the bottom to obtain the most effective presentation. Adjustments in leader length should be made.

The downstream nymphing style of fly fishing provides the angler with an interesting method of presentation and is a technique that at times demands a high degree of alertness from the fly fisherman in order to detect the acceptance of his offering.

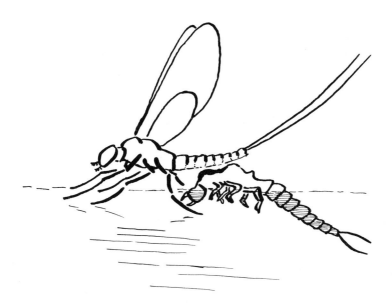

CHAPTER 14

Surface-Film Fishing Techniques

THE BORDERLINE OF WET AND DRY

The most recent important development in fly-fishing technique is the fishing of the feathered offering in the surface film — not quite the traditional dry-fly style, nor exactly wet-fly fishing either. You will recall that where the areas of wet fly and nymph overlapped, the word "flymph" was the resulting terminology, so "drymph" could as easily be applied to the borderline of nymph and dry-fly styles.

A floating line is used to fish the fly in the regions of the surface film. The leader too is greased to ride on the top, save for the final four to eight inches of the tippet, which is required to sink. It is a method of fishing a fly that provides an enormous amount of angling pleasure and demands the ultimate in expertise and concentration on the part of the fly fisherman.

The object of the angling form is to offer the fly as the suggestion of a creature trapped in the topmost section of the water, or of an emerging insect in the upper layer of the stream. An acceptance of the deceiving morsel of steel, fur, and feather — seen when the fish breaks water, as the fly is taken when it lies in the surface film — produces a bulging, wave-pushing rise form. At other times, when the fly is suspended two or three inches below the surface, the take is often not visually detectable and carrying modernisms to extremes, the take is a mixture of both the rise and the strike, so what possibly occurs could be named a "strise" . . . .

From my experience the best time to try this method is at dusk, casting upstream at a slight angle, using a light line outfit on a smooth glide at the tail or head of a pool, where the water depth ranges from four to twelve inches. These are spots which generally during daylight hours are almost impossible to approach without disturbing the fish that have adopted feeding stations in them, but which at dusk can be approached easily. In the evening they invariably hold some of the larger denizens that have been hidden within the still depths while the sun was on the water.

156

Upstream techniques

The angling cast is made using the proven technique for upstream fly fishing in fast-flowing current: three rod lengths of line, placed on the water with a soft, low delivery. It is imperative that there be good co-ordination of the hand strip-back of line and rod-lift to keep in contact with the fly.

Even at dusk a smooth, unbroken glide always retains a sheen of light upon which the floating line can be discerned and, if the correct casting procedures are observed (the rod dictating direction and the line following the course of the delivery), the line will be seen on the water immediately the cast is executed by looking along the rod, for the line will be extended straight ahead of it. The angling method demands that the area where the fly is carried by the current, a leader length above the end of the line, be watched closely and the fisherman, with maximum attention, be poised to tighten on should the line deviate in any way from the drift speed provided by the current flow, and be on the alert for a tell-tale swirl if it occurs in the general area that contains the fly. Then, by lifting the rod slightly, draw the line taut — an action that ensures that the barb will find its mark; the fish being positioned above the angler. When the offering is taken, a downstream pull sets the hook firmly.

The method has a rather curious aspect concerning the acceptance of the fly, in that the offering is taken so unsuspectingly that when the rise is seen, the size of the disturbance made on the surface of the water is absolutely no guide to the size of the fish. The take, when using this technique, can possibly be rated as one of the quietest, most deliberate, and positive acceptances of the fly that the angler will encounter. Light conditions in the late evening will often make the style difficult to use, but if the angler crouches low or kneels in the stream, the line can often be seen. There are not many sights in angling with the fly more thrilling and satisfying than to see the water erupt in a silent unbroken mound as the offering in the surface film is taken, knowing that only a drawing tight of the line is all that is needed to establish a positive connection with the fish.

Downstream techniques

Although emphasis has been placed on the upstream style of surface film fishing, there are certain downstream methods which can produce fish when angling conditions are difficult. Take, for example, a long flat shaded by overhanging trees during the height of summer when rivers are low and the water runs clear and slow. This is the typical place where fish congregate, as there is likely to be a good supply of food available and the environment offers safety because it provides good visual and sensory warnings of danger.

A little time should be spent in preparation before attempting to fish such a spot. It should first be determined what section of the stretch the piscine quarry favors. Reconnoiter the area to decide the best position for casting — above the spot that holds the fish. Then retire for fifteen minutes or so. During this period, the line should be stripped from the reel (best done by hooking the fly to the branch of a tree and walking twenty yards allowing the reel to pay-off line) and the line rubbed down with floatant to ensure that it sits high in the water. The leader too, should be treated — all but the final six inches — tested and checked for wind knots, and the hook examined.

When all this has been done, and the line is once more stored on the reel, a cautious approach should be made to the spot selected to present the fly. The cast, which has two phases, is made almost directly across the river and, with luck, there may be sufficient space to execute an aerialized cast. If not, a series of gentle roll casts will have to be made to extend the line, which completes Phase One of the cast. If there is no casting space whatsoever, the second phase is used. (At this point I would stress that care must be taken to choose a place that enables a fish to be landed as well as a cast to be made.) Phase Two is achieved by stripping line from the reel and allowing the slow flow of the current to drift the line downstream. This technique, when applied to the casts thrown across the stream, permits the line to slowly swing on a lenghtened course across the river.

The elongated journey that is given to the feathered offering can be made more attractive by holding the line back an instant (not enough to cause a wake with the line) which is an action that lifts the fly higher in the surface film and, when the line is released, causes the fly to sink a little deeper. When this technique is employed, a take is best detected by watching the end of the line (some anglers attach a marker, such as a piece of bright wool) which, when it stabs underwater, provides the signal to tighten on.

"Hyper" Tackle

Another branch of this style of fly fishing is the method which embraces the use of "hyper" tackle: tiny flies, gossamer tippets, extra-light lines, and ultra-fine, soft-action rods with minimal power ratings. The very small flies imitate midge pupa and other micro-morsels that fish occasionally prefer above all else, and such minute hooks necessitate the use of fine leaders. The light lines provide the most gentle presentation, and the low power rods are needed to cushion the leader against breakage when playing a fish on such light tackle. Sometimes really large specimens are taken with this equipment.

Occasionally fish can be selective when feeding, but for most of the time they exist mainly on a mixed diet of forage food taken from the surface and

158

below. The object when fishing the fly in this style is to suggest a food form by the method of presentation, and the slight halting of the line as the fly is slowly drifted downstream has the effect of simulating a waterlogged fly or an emerging insect.

CHAPTER 15

The Dry Fly

THE FLOATED OFFERING

Dry-fly fishing is the method of angling with the fly rod where, as the name implies, the presentation of the feathered offering is made upon the surface of the water, and the acceptance of the fly — the rise — is detected visually by the angler. It is a style of fly fishing that has probably had more written about it than any other branch of the sport.

In the following sections which deal with this aspect of fly rodding, only the basic details of the angling form will be outlined, for the chapters are intended solely as an introduction and a starting point from which fishermen may base their own angling experience and investigation.

The traditional method of dry-fly fishing evolved when flies were actually tied to float, during the middle of late nineteenth century, in southern England. It was here that the classic Halford theory of presentation was born: the upstream cast; the avoidance of drag; the dead drift. The dry fly, in its truest sense, is intended to imitate the natural insect floating on the water, and the interest generated by this angling form in those early days has continued to fascinate fly fishermen ever since. The challenge is to present the fly in a manner which the fish accepts, by placing and manipulating the line over the water flow so that the pull of the current on the line does not drag the fly across the surface in an unnatural way (causing a "V" wake), and by using a fly, the dressing of which represents as closely as possible the insects floating on the stream.

To see a fish rise to the surface and accept the floating offering without hesitation, is a moment that rates high with fly fishermen, and the visual thrill of the angling method is probably one of the main reasons for the large number of fishermen the technique has gathered around it over the years, championed by Halford in Britain, and anglers such as Hewitt in North America.

To fully explain the rudimentary style of dry-fly fishing, it is best to return to the simplified definition of the two methods — wet, searching the water

160

for a fish inclined to take the fly; while with the dry, a feeding fish is stalked. To expand the dry technique a little further, "fishing the water", is the term applied to casting the dry fly to spots likely to hold fish, and "fishing the rise", is when the fly is presented to a feeding fish.

The dry fly is attached to a long tapered leader, between seven and eighteen feet long, and the feathered offering is dressed in a size, shape, and form that imitate a floating insect similar to those upon which the fish are feeding or are likely to take. When fishing the dry fly, the line, the fly, and all but the last six or eight inches of the fine leader tippet must float. The reason for the final section of the leader next to the fly to be sunk is that the shadow of the floating tippet creates an unnatural impression. A floating tippet is often the cause of a refusal at the last instant. A sunk tippet eliminates this condition.

With the upstream method of fly fishing, the line is cast at an angle, up and across the water flow, as was the procedure with the other angling forms that have been described. However, before the cast is executed, a close scrutiny of the main and secondary currents is necessary for subtleties of surface speed and the complexeties of directional flow and pace directly affect the behavior of the offering. The object of the cast is to allow the fly to drift downstream over the selected spot (chosen because a feeding fish was seen to rise or because the place looked likely to hold a fish) on the surface in a natural manner. As the line is lying across the current flow with its varied stream speeds, the angler must lay the line at the angle that will aid the lifelike float which is desired — care being taken that the line does not cover the fish before the fly — and the fisherman must deposit the line on the surface in a manner that will assist the natural presentation of the fly during the course of the drift. Finally, there has to be an element of accuracy and finesse in the delivery of the line when it is put in the water. A heavy presentational delivery is certain to disturb the fish and must be avoided at all costs. A clumsy cast signals to the fish that something is amiss.

Ideally, the fly should be cast delicately, well above the feeding position, fractionally to the side so that the fly is the closest part of the tackle to the fish and, should the offering be ignored, the line picked off the water well below (done by producing a high delivery of the roll cast, that creates an aerialized frontal delivery, so picking the fly cleanly from the water) and then the line taken to the rear with the normal backcast.

There is a great deal of false-casting done when the floating offering is being fished, partly to dry off the fly and partly to keep a workable length of line in operation while determining where to place the delivery. Most of the time it is just as easy when changing location to keep the line pumping back and forth in the air as it is to reel in the line, and it has the advantage of keeping the angler immediately "operational," should a rise be spotted.

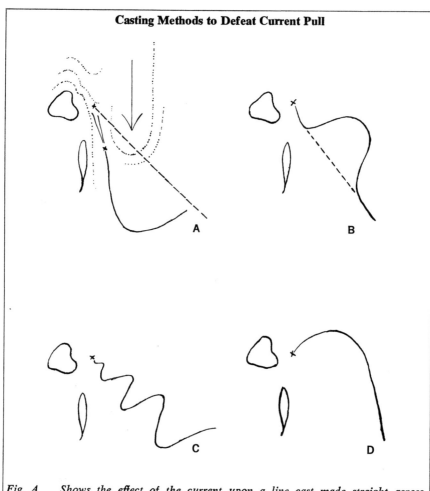

Casting Methods to Defeat Current Pull

Fig. A   Shows the effect of the current upon a line cast made straight across the stream.

Fig. B   The same cast is made, then a corrective upstream mend is executed.

Fig. C   The loose line cast snaked over the current is achieved by a high delivery, and the rod waved from side to side as the line extends.

Fig. D   An example of the curved cast, the result of an under or over-energized delivery.

In fast, broken water, a more buoyant fly is needed than is required for glide sections which flow smoothly and offer greater surface tension to support less heavily dressed offerings. For choppy water, more hackles, hair, or fiber wings and bodies created from deer-body hair are dressing methods which provide the fly with greater buoyancy and are favored fly types for rough water.

For dry-fly work the rod is generally held on a higher angle than in the other forms of fly fishing in order to lift as much of the line clear of the surface (and so avoid contact with the flow to minimize drag) as possible.

After the initial presentation of the fly, drag is the major problem which faces the fisherman, and it is only with practice and experience that the angler will overcome the difficulty of counteracting the flow pattern by line placement. However, by using casting techniques that enable him to deposit loose line (snakes), bends and curves (under and over-energized deliveries), and mends (derived from the roll cast, where a bag of line is thrown above or below the fly) all help nullify the effect of the uneven speeds of the current on the line.

FISHING THE DRY FLY

The traditional method of fishing the floated offering was to cast the fly upstream, and endeavor to place and control the line so as to produce a "perfect drift." The object was to present the fly without drag and show the buoyant offering in an absolutely motionless manner, save for the progress provided by the flow of the current.

Technique has changed somewhat since those early days, and tackle has been tremendously refined, although the drag problem remains constant. There have, however, evolved new styles of fishing the fly, and the so-called "dead drift" has been embellished with subtle forms of life suggestion by rod movement. Actions which inject the fly with tiny flickers of movement, that simulate a resettling of position by the insect, or make the deceiving morsel emit what could be a minute flicker of wing motion, give the offering a great deal more authenticity and result in a more ready acceptance by the fish.

Some insects are quite active upon the surface of the water and, by the skillful use of rod manipulation, the actions they perform can be imitated very realistically. Caddis flies, for example, skate across the water with short bursts of speed, leaving small "V" lines in the surface film behind them, which can be reproduced by adroit use of the fly rod. Larger creatures such as grasshoppers struggle really vigorously to escape the pull of the current and, by tapping the rod with the finger if the line is taut from tip to fly, small vibratory rings can be made to radiate from the imitation used by the angler. The suggestion of life, achieved below the surface by the wet-fly angler from teasing rod action and soft breathing motion of the materials from which the sunk fly is made, is now integrated into modern dry-fly technique and is produced by rod manipulation. A dry fly can be made to skate or flicker, twitch or flutter, and the method of transmitting the suggestion of living motion to the floating offering has increased the angling potential of the fishing style enormously.

This method is not easily employed in fast, broken water. However, on smooth-flowing stretches (from quick glides to slow-moving pools) the style will produce a rise to the fly when a "dead drift" type of presentation would be totally ignored.

I first used the struggling insect technique many years ago, fishing the floating fly on a stretch of water that during daylight hours was quite unsuited for fly fishing — a deep, slow-moving section of water above a dam. The stretch was canal-like and was contained within low grass-hung banks that at dusk were the surface feeding areas of the large fish that inhabited the deep slow-moving water. Some anglers who fished the place occasionally caught them by patiently dapping with a live fly (the "quick" fly as described by Walton) — by suspending the natural on to the water along the overhung edges of the section and waiting for a hungry fish to discover it. The method I devised was to lower the artificial — a bushy spider pattern was my favorite — and only a few inches of the leader on to the water and, rather than wait for a cruising fish to find it, "advertise" its presence by tapping the rod with my finger. The staccato drumming vibrating through the rod and down the line caused tiny rings to emit from the fly and encircle the offering on the surface in the same manner as that produced by a trapped insect. The result was that fish, searching for food, identified the disturbance as some edible creature caught in the surface film and came directly to the feathered deceiver and accepted it without hesitation. One important lesson I did learn from the exercise was not to tighten on when the rise was seen, but to allow the few inches of loose leader to be pulled tight to the rod and let the weight of the fish drive the hook home. To pull up the rod when the fish was seen to break surface was fatal — there being no contact with the fish at all — and the only certain way of hooking it was to allow the four inches of slack to do the work.

Dapping is the term used when the fly is fished suspended from the rod to the surface without the line being in contact with the water. The method is employed mainly in Ireland and Scotland on fishing lakes (loughs and lochs respectively), using long rods that are held upright. The wind is allowed to blow the line which enables the fisherman to make the fly skip across the waves. It is imperative that a rise to the fly, when fished by the dapping method, be granted a slight pause before the action of tightening on is attempted, or there will be no contact with the fish. This rise type, together with the fact that the line is not touching the water, necessitates a short delay before the line is drawn tight to hook the fish.

PRESENTATION

Lightweight hooks and new dressing materials have given the feathered offering added sophistication, better performance, and greater potential. There are, however, certain pitfalls to be avoided: hooks can be shielded by bulky, buoyant bodies; barbs can be masked with bushy hackles; elon-

Dry-Fly Presentational Methods

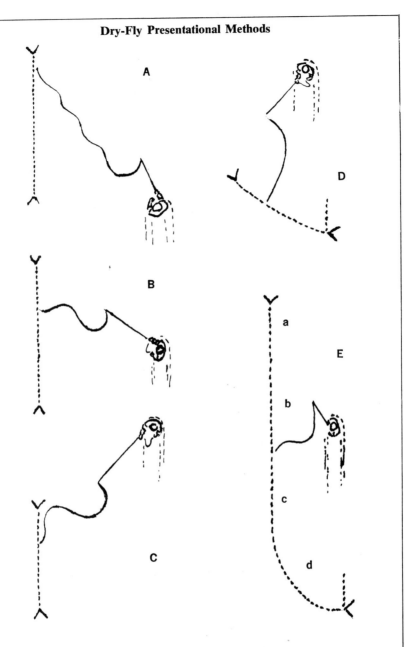

Fig. A   *Shows the traditional upstream dry-fly approach.*
Fig. B   *Depicts the view from above of the segmented up-and-below style of drift.*
Fig. C   *The downstream float*
Fig. D   *Cross-current swing that skates the fly over the flow*
Fig. E   *The modern technique which integrates the four methods into one long drift*

gated bodies that contribute little to the effectiveness of the fly tend to hinder good hook penetration; over-long hook shanks do not assist contact. The standard length shank, wide gape hook, is undoubtedly the best.

Possibly the most-used angling technique with the floating offering by the contemporary dry-fly fisherman is a combination of four methods: the upstream approach, the downstream drift, an overlapping of these two styles where the cast is less severely angled and the float starts above and finishes below the angler, and a variation of the downstream presentation which allows the fly to swing across the surface and produces a skating action from the offering. Skate is not drag. Drag describes the condition when the fly is pulled down the stream by a line captured by the current creating an effect where the fly looks like a miniature speedboat. Skate is a situation where the fly dances across the stream, and the angler controls the action of the feathered artifice. These four proven methods, each a successful individual angling style, when integrated and embellished with the living-motion technique, provide the modern angler with very potent forms of surface presentation.

The procedure when using this grand slam dry-fly presentation (best executed on long slow glides), is achieved in the following manner: first the normal stages of the angled upstream cast are observed. However, as the fly approaches the point where a pick-off would occur, the rod is held high and what would be the second segment of "up and below" drift is executed; then the line which was retrieved on the downstream journey is fed into a downward drift. When the full extent of the downstream float has been reached, the fly is skated and danced across the flow and, finally, skipped back a few feet before being picked off and another cast made.

The visual acceptance of the feathered offering, the rise to the dry fly, is the signal for the angler to draw the line taut, which enables the hook to find a hold. This final act, however, is a constant enigma as there are many factors involved: the size of the fish, which governs the quickness or deliberation of the take: the flow rate of the current which influences the speed of the feeding action: the angle of the fish to the angler (the fish turning towards or away from the fisherman) on acceptance: all must be instantly decided, and then the tightening executed.

Rod length and action for dry-fly work is one of personal choice. However, a longer rod has definite advantages as fly manipulation and line control are performed more easily and the tightening of the line to make contact with a fish is achieved with less effort.

To provide the reader with still greater awareness of the necessity of recognizing rise forms, here are two examples: first, a fast rise, made at an acute angle by the fish to the fly on the surface causes a noisy "glop" sound, and requires a fast lift of the rod tip to connect with the fish: second, a slow "sipped" rise made on exactly the same angle creates a silent dimple of acceptance, and the fisherman replies with a slower tightening of the line.

It is best that the water be studied with these aspects in mind so that rise types may be anticipated in conjunction with the evaluation of line-drift problems and, although one can only generalize on procedure where the acceptance of the fly is concerned, a guide of operation can be based on a rule: the faster the rise, the quicker the tightening action becomes. Occasionally a pulling stroke to the side with the rod is better than a lifting action. There is an instinctive element of timing which develops when fishing the dry fly, and a recognition of rise form which automatically registers and to which the angler reacts almost unthinkingly — the rise is seen, identified, he tightens on.

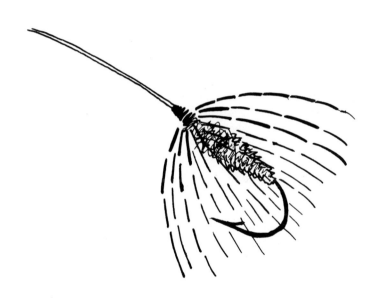

CHAPTER 16

Techniques for Small Streams

The opportunity to put into practice every phase of fly-fishing skill is presented to the angler when he is confronted with the smaller stream, for here every possible angling situation can be contained within a few hundred yards of water. Although lacking the volume of flow, and devoid of a big area of fishable water, what the smaller stream lacks in size is compensated by character, for here will be found in miniature, pools and glides, rifflles and tumbles, flats and rapids which, in such reduced circumstances, demand a high level of angling expertise before any success can be experienced.

Residents of such small confines are invariably wary and are much harder to catch than the denizens of larger bodies of water, but it is this test that makes the fishing of such small streams a delightful experience. Progress must be stealthy and attention must be given to movement and shadow: false casts should be made to the side of the spot where the fly is to be placed as the fine spray that is thrown from the line and the fly is often sufficient to send a fish darting for cover.

Small dry-fly glides, tiny wet-fly riffles, diminutive nymphing slicks, and minute back eddies, that lie to the side of rocks and substitute for the boulders of more powerful streams can be searched with a streamer. Bushes overhang stretches where normally trees would lattice larger waterways, yet the drifted dry fly floated beneath the canopy of branches and the line drawn tight when a rise is audibly detected, is a technique that will produce fish.

If the upstream method of dry-fly fishing is employed, the degree of finesse and accuracy required is extremely high, and the presentational factor demands that casts be precise and the tackle handling of the highest order. On a large river the line can be put upon the water in a general area. However, on small streams, inches make the difference between a drift that will have acceptance and a float that will be ignored. Casts which place the fly tight alongside a half-submerged log, undercut banks, and slabbed rock formations, are the drifts that will produce a take.

Due to the smallness of the angling venue, the stream is easy to read and locations that will hold fish are easily recognizable. Here the technique of "fishing the water" becomes tremendously interesting, for the dry fly can be used to create a hatch of flies. The method of drifting the fly several times over a specific area has the effect of suggesting to the fish that a number of insects are floating downstream and will often stimulate a feeding impulse that will result in a rise.

With the nymph and wet fly, both the upstream and downstream methods can be used to good effect. I have been introduced to a rather innovative, North American style of nymph fishing that will take fish from deeper, slow-moving sections that would be difficult to fish by other methods. The technique requires that the nymph be contained inside a small lump of moist earth and dropped gently into the water. When the nymph concealed in the mud sinks to the bottom, the water causes the soil to disintegrate and, if the line is drawn up with a Leisenring Lift, there is created the condition exactly like a pupa breaking free of the stream bed, abandoning its nymphal shuck, and starting its emergent journey to the surface.

Like many others, I learnt my craft as a boy on smaller streams and was shown a style of angling that has proved its worth time and time again by an old mine worker who took me into his confidence. Amos was a fine old fellow and I recall one summer when I was about thirteen years of age, he being retired and I on vacation from school, we fished together many times. On one occasion there had been heavy rain the day previously and we found the stream running high and mud colored. My feelings of disappointment at finding the water so unsuited to fly fishing turned to amazement as my elderly companion smiled at me and started to assemble his equipment. Heading upstream and passing spots that we normally would have fished had the water been lower, we stopped at a pool below some rapids where several small grassy promontories jutted out into the flow, behind each of which was a foam-covered backwater.

Amos attached a dark, bushy dry fly and, using only a rod length of line, dropped the fly on to the foam and gave the fly a twitch. A fish immediately took the fly, was hooked, and landed. The same thing occurred at the next patch of foam. When my turn came, I succeeded in getting a rise but did not hook the fish because my immediate and involuntary action was to jerk up the rod, a move causing my companion to chuckle loudly. I remember I did hook the third or fourth offer that my fly received and, with Amos accompanying me, watching, and giving advice, we searched for and fished the patches of foam. Fish look for the safety of cover, and the opaque roof that foam provides is ideal habitat for them. Foam invariably collects on backwaters, and such eddies are accumulation points of piscine food; normally when there is foam there will be fish.

When fly fishing on small streams the amount of line used averages two or three rod lengths and the casting area is normally restricted, which means that the rod movement is executed on all planes. Also, the roll cast is at times a valuable asset to place the fly in a spot that is unreachable with an aerialized cast. Delicacy of presentation, together with careful line extension and control, dictates that the normal methods used for larger waters be refined to suit the miniature conditions that in a reverse way seem to magnify the difficulties of presenting the fly.

Stretches overhung with grass or bushes, areas where fish are conditioned to insects falling into the water, and on small streams, a dapping style of fly fishing can be done, or casts can be made so that the fly hits the bank and then tumbles on to the water. There is also an interesting and realistic effect created when the fly is first cast on to the grass and then pulled to drop to the surface. One point that should be stressed is that the fly ought to be delivered from such a position that a fish may be landed, as occasionally the determination to deposit the fly in a particular spot is compromised by the fact that the rod and casting arm have been maneuvered through a gap in trees, so that when a fish is attached to the line, movement and the landing of the quarry are an impossibility.

It is generally thought that small streams require short rods, but from my experience I have found rods less than six feet in length not as useful as those six inches either side of seven feet. The challenge of fishing small waters, the world over, be they known as burn, beck or brook, feeder or creek, stream or tributary, occupies a special place in angling venues ánd are in many ways the supreme test to the skill and ingenuity of the fly fisherman.

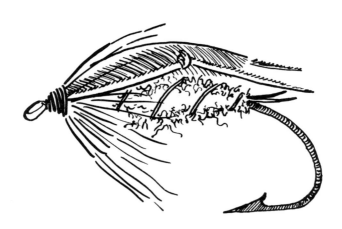

CHAPTER 17

Techniques for Fishing
Still Water

In the descriptions of the previous methods of fishing the fly, with the exception of the brief mention of the stationary dry fly, the flow of the current has played an important role. In bodies of water that lack movement — lakes, ponds, and reservoirs — the angler must provide the motion.

Casting ability, angling prowess, and fishing skill are the necessary requisites which make the successful still-water angler. At any time top-class lake anglers are capable of producing the delicate short-line presentation of the chalk stream, the long line method of the steelhead angler, the adroit recovery of the nymph fisherman, combined with the purposeful approach of the sea-trout specialist, and the tenacity of the salmon angler. Quite possibly good still-water fly fishermen represent the best all-around performers with a fly rod to be found anywhere.

When fishing large areas of water from the bank, the farther an angler can cast, the more water can be searched with the fly, and the greater will be his chances of success. It is the fly fishermen who choose to fish still water who have recognized the usefulness of the shooting head line and adopted the hauling method technique of casting to achieve greater distance. They select their equipment from a casting performance aspect and they, more than other fly fishermen, take full advantage of the various densities of lines that are available to make their style more efficient.

Sunk-fly methods, streamer, nymph, and wet fly are the main fish-producing styles of still-water fly fishing. However, as was stated previously, the fly after being cast out, as the water is static, must be retrieved to create the suggestion of life or attract the attention of the piscine quarry and, during the process of recovery, manipulated to simulate a living motion. The speed and depth of recovery, together with the method of retrieve govern the degree of acceptance of the fly.

Unlike fish species in moving water that adopt favorable positions within the flow, fish in still water move about quite freely, although they do at times lie dormant. In any body of still water there are areas where fish tend to congregate, influenced no doubt by comfort factors such as food sources, water temperature, and cover. In most large areas of still water fifty per cent of the fishing area produces ninety-five percent of the total number of fish caught, and it is the task of the still-water fly fisherman to recognize and find these areas.

The angler can cover more water fishing from a boat, by drifting with the wind and then anchoring when an area where fish are feeding is discovered. However, the methods to be discussed will be described from the bank fisherman's approach but can be easily adapted to boat fishing. First let me comment briefly on safety and casting etiquette in a boat. Unless the boat is large enough and sufficiently stable to support a standing angler, cast and land fish from a sitting position; if two anglers are fishing from the same craft, cast with the lines aerialized away from the confines of the boat; should three fishermen be casting, the most accomplished user of the equipment is placed in the middle, and the lines are cast in rotation.

Unless there is visible feeding activity on the surface, the objective of the still-water fly fisherman is to discover what the fish will accept — wet fly, nymph, or streamer. All the methods of fly fishing that have been dealt with up to this point can be used to good effect. However, the major difference

---

Line Function in Still Water

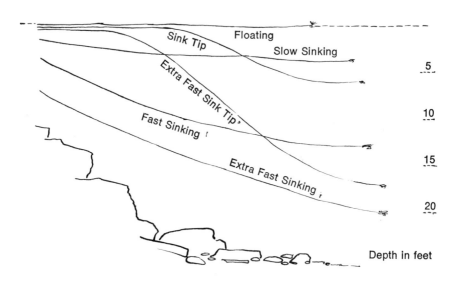

is that, whereas the current flow aided the presentation and assisted the coverage of the stream with the fly, on still water the fisherman must cast out the fly and then by the method of retrieve, inject some suggestion of life or an element of attraction to the feathered offering by the style of line recovery.

Before equipment reached present-day levels of casting performance, the drawing back of line was done by a manipulative hand method, which allowed the fisherman to hold in his palm several yards of line, while the fingers of the hand were used to pull in the line a few tantalizing inches at a time (the other hand gripped the rod and ultimately controlled the line by forefinger pressure). Today, with casting distances increased tremendously, (although if short casts are made, the hand-storage retrieve style is still used) when perhaps twenty-five to thirty yards of line must be recovered, the line is stripped back and deposited to the side of the fisherman either on the water, into the boat, on the ground, or into a tray-like container strapped to the waist of the angler (a stripping and shooting basket). This latter system is an innovative method of line storage used by steelhead and still-water fly fishermen to increase angling and casting efficiency.

Casting Positions in a Boat

Water temperature greatly influences the activity pattern of subaqueous creatures in both still and moving water. Extremes of heat and cold cause fish to become lethargic and less inclined to feed. However, if the fly fisherman experiments with the type of offering, the angling method, and his fishing technique, there is always a good chance of making contact.

The speed, depth, and recovery style of the feathered offering, and the manner in which it is fished, are the factors which influence to a great degree the success of the still-water fly fisherman. Wet flies and nymph imitations can be fished back very slowly in the surface film, or crawled over the bottom; drawn back quite briskly in mid-water or jumped across the lake bed with short bursts of motion; pulled back with a lazy sink and draw action; or allowed to sink, while giving a couple of sharp twitches to attract attention, and then lifted upwards to the surface.

It is best to hold the rod low to the water at an oblique angle to the direction of the line when fly-fishing still water, as this procedure gives the angler more control of the fly to either lift it or to drive the hook positively home. It also governs the upward course the line follows on the retrieve: should a really large fish strike the fly, the side position of the rod to the direction of the take cushions the impact exerted on the tippet. If the rod were pointing straight down the line, the initial shock would be taken by the leader.

Exciting still-water fishing can be had with the dry fly, but the angler must realize that he is casting to cruising fish (as opposed to the situation in moving water, where generally the fish is stationary and is feeding on food items drifting over it). The living motion methods of twitching the fly to attract attention and simulate life, together with the skating styles of presentation, can be most productive at times. Here again, the speed of the rise is the factor that guides the angler as to the speed of his drawing tight the line.

Flies presented in the upper layers of the water and in the surface film are more successful for evening still-water fly fishing, due to the limitation of visibility which occurs at dusk.

Fishing the streamer in still water is an aspect of fly fishing that I find completely absorbing. I attempt to present it as a bait-fish imitation and attractor and fish it accordingly. There is a behavioral pattern among fish which is most interesting — should an item be the cause of slight curiosity or a mild hunger stimulus, it can be brought to a peak by taking it on a sudden curved path of flight away from the interested piscine observer. This motion will cause an equally fast reaction from the predator and create a situation whereby the bait will be taken.

The method I have devised to take advantage of this situation is to cast the fly as far out as possible, deposit ten or twelve feet of extra line on to the water, as I walk along the bank for three or four yards, and then start the recovery procedure. The most successful retrieve pattern is a fast darting pull with slight pauses and, if there has been no strike on the way in, it can be expected to occur as the line swings obliquely to the bank simulating the sudden curved path of flight. A fly line will attempt to follow faithfully the form it had when it was laid upon the water (a reason why trolling with a fly from a boat is so successful around jutted shores and bays) and the directional change method I have detailed will produce a strike from fish who so irritatingly repeatedly follow the fly inshore, occasionally plucking at the tail of the fly.

Line handling on still water is the secret of attracting fish to the fly, and if my verbal treatment of technique such as making the fly jump, hop, flutter, skate, crawl, dart and race for the surface and terms such as extracting a teasing motion by vibrating and rocking the rod are understood by the reader, then I have succeeded in passing over sound information regarding the method of fishing a fly.

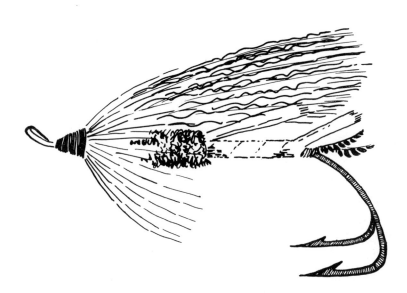

CHAPTER 18

Atlantic Salmon Fishing

The Atlantic Salmon is an anadromous species; it spawns in fresh water, and then, as a three-year old moves to salt water, returning once more to the river from the sea as a mature fish at five or six years of age to spawn, and perhaps return to the sea. It is unlike the Pacific Salmon which dies after spawning.

My advice to experienced fly fishermen who intend fishing for salmon for the first time is to put from their minds the presentational skills they have developed from other aspects of fly fishing, where the feathered offering is used to imitate aquatic creatures, bait fish, and insects. This may sound rather melodramatic, but it is possibly the best way to impress upon anglers new to salmon fly fishing that there is a considerable difference between the skills required for salmon fishing and those that are employed for all other forms of fly fishing. The Atlantic Salmon does not feed in fresh water after its return to the river from the sea and yet it can be taken with a fly. A theory held by many is that the feathered offering provokes a feeding reflex associated with the initial period of the life cycle spent in fresh water.

FAVORED HABITAT

Salmon tend to favor certain sections of the river and they adopt these same lies season after season. The reason why some pools hold the migratory fish and others do not, poses intriguing possibilities. I was told some years ago of studies done on the River Spey in Scotland that analyzed the situation in the following manner: the preferred sections of river contained moving water over three feet in depth and had a bed consisting of a combination of rock shelves, gravel, pebbles, and stones up to the size of a man's fist, and rock ledges and boulders larger than two feet in diameter. Sections that did not hold fish were deep sluggish-flowing stretches, shallows without cover, and areas that consisted of rocks ranging from grapefruit size to large melons.

It was this last condition that was considered to hold the clue to the habitat most favored by the anadromous fish: the composition of the river bed. Medium-sized rocks cause the water flow beneath the surface to move in turbulent layers which batter and pummel the fish, causing sufficient discomfort for salmon to avoid resting in such areas. The composition of the river bed, combined with the current speed, govern the form of layer flow and stream force by frictional contact, which perhaps explains why fish change positions in high water and move location in low conditions, while other stretches only hold fish at certain water heights. The results of the investigation done on the Spey pointed emphatically to the fact that salmon show a decided preference to areas of the river that have a bed structure that provides an even current flow.

As salmon do not feed in fresh water after they return to the river from the sea, the offering of the fly fisherman under these circumstances can be viewed only as an attractor, provoking an element of anger, curiosity, or perhaps touching upon some past feeding impulse. Whatever may be the reason for the stimulus, the fish provides tremendous sport for the fly fisherman, and is given top honors by some anglers above even steelhead (anadromous rainbow trout), tarpon, bass, and trout.

Reference to the fly size, leader strengths, line weight, and rod power-charts, earlier in the book will re-familiarize the reader with the tackle used for salmon fly fishing. The methods to be outlined apply to both single and two-handed fly rods.

Described below are the various methods of salmon fly fishing dealt with as though being used on a specific stretch of river. The section is fabricated to rekindle the memories of everyone who has fished for salmon and will be a test for the imagination of anglers who have yet to experience the angling form as a typical salmon resting place (lie).

On the far bank, the bedrock shows below the earth and reaches steeply up to the trees that overlook the pool; the rock slopes into the river in shelving steps, visible near the surface, and then becomes more steeply angled and disappears into the green depths. Above the fisherman, the head of the pool merges with the gliding tail of the section upstream from where the angler stands. The river narrows, gains speed and gushes through a contracted throat in turbulent rapids split by a huge rock. As the pool widens the flow is smoothed, the river at the far shore contained by the rock face is shouldered away leaving a trace of hesitant backwater which spreads towards the angler up an inclined gravel bank. Below the fisherman the pace of the water slows, flows into the main body of the pool, and then quickens into the tail glide which, because of large boulders, is quickly broken, slicked, and riffled, pouring down rapids which head the next stretch of the river.

The pool tapers rapidly in depth from two feet to four, from where the current is split by the rock, and then more gradually to perhaps a depth of fifteen feet in the slow-moving body of the pool, then again shallowing to only a foot or so in the swift tailwater.

Salmon will occasionally display themselves by leaping clear of the water, and the actions they produce are worthy of discussion. A "boiling" surface disturbance, "rolls" and a "head and tail" motion breaking the water are encouraging signs for an angler to detect, as such fish will show interest in the fly. However, an almost vertical leap and an ungraceful, splashing fallback has, in my experience, never been a good omen as far as the acceptance of my fly has been concerned. Jumping in the tails of pools and immediately below rapids are normally actions produced by salmon running upstream and at such times they are not interested in any offering the fly fisherman may place before them.

An angler who lacks the expertise in salmon-fishing technique, and is unaware of the angling method that is necessary to get an acceptance, will often observe a fish jumping and will start fishing directly opposite where he saw the disturbance, casting his fly to the precise spot he saw the fish break water. This procedure is not correct for several reasons: the fish does not lie directly below the place the rise occurred (often a salmon moves on an upward course of many feet before the leap), and the presentational aspects of the salmon fly dictate that the offering be shown to the fish by the angler casting from above the location, and presented on a taut line in order to attract the attention of the fish to the fly.

SALMON FLIES

The fly used for salmon fishing, during the progress of its development, reached its peak of grandeur in the late nineteenth century, with really ornate dressings created from all manner of exotic materials. Flies for modern salmon fishing are not so complex in design, as many of the rare birds that provided feathers for the creation of the traditional flies are now protected, and tying them is becoming a dying art. Hair is now more commonly used in the construction of the wings, and bodies are gradually becoming less complicated. Great importance was once given to the building of the feathered wing and numerous strips of contrasting feathers were married into beautiful offerings that were truly works of art. Salmon flies tied in the early 1900's are prized as possessions to cherish, rather than fish with.

The modern salmon fly, although lacking the decorative appearance of the old-time variety, is equally effective. Flies are tied on both single and double irons: a single hook is lighter and rides higher in the water than the double. Some anglers favor the single hook, which behaves rather like a yacht in the current, the wing being tipped by the flow like a sail and the bend of the hook acting as a keel, which has the effect of showing two silhouettes to the salmon. Other fishermen prefer the double hook, as it fishes more deeply, and there is the attraction of the hooking potential. The twin irons, however, can also offer twice the leverage and, in situations where one hook is exposed, the salmon can lever the hold free on a rock. Both hook types have their advocates. It is a matter of personal choice as to which is used.

There are a great many salmon fly dressings, too numerous to detail in a work of this nature. Furthermore, the patterns salmon prefer vary from river to river, although some fly dressings have become synonomous with the sport: Jock Scott, Green Highlander, Dusty Miller, Thunder and Lightning, Silver Wilkinson, Black Doctor, Blue Charm, Garry, Hairy Mary, Durham Ranger, and Yellow Torrish, all from Britain; from North America, Rusty Rat, Black Dose, Black Bomber, Red Abbey, Orange Blossom, Grizzly King, Butterfly, Cosseboom, Green Butt, Grey Wulff, Whiskers, and Rat-Faced MacDougall. All these serve the angler well.

The colors of these patterns vary, and for some reason, salmon in a specific river will show a decided preference for certain patterns. The size of the offering also plays an important role.

An angler would be well advised to determine when he plans his trip what patterns, hook types, and sizes of fly are used on the river at the time he intends to visit it, as they control to a certain extent the degree of success the fisherman may expect to encounter. The methods of salmon fly fishing remain reasonably constant. The same cannot be said of the offering — pattern and size vary considerably from river to river.

BASIC METHODS OF SALMON FLY FISHING

The typical salmon pool detailed in the preceding section will be the location on which the various styles of fishing the fly will be described, and the pattern and size, although not under discussion could be a 6/0 Silver Wilkinson in Norway, a Size 4 Rusty Rat in New Brunswick, a Size 8 Hairy Mary in Scotland, a 2/0 Optic Chillimps in Sweden, a tiny Size 12 double Jock Scott in Iceland, a Size 6 Brown Bomber in Labrador, or a Size 2 Dusty Miller in Ireland; embraced under the mantle of the old rules which are: bright day — dark fly; dull day — light fly: big fly — high water; small fly — low water.

Salmon can be taken with both the sunk (wet) and the floating (dry) offering, and the fishing of the wet fly will be discussed first. There are two distinct styles contained in the wet fly method — deeply sunk presentations, and techniques that offer the fly in the upper layer of the water.

The Deeply Sunk Fly

Dealing first with the deeply sunk wet fly, the modern sinking lines have made this presentational style highly efficient for early-season fishing when

179

Heavy lines show the angle of the cast when fishing the deeply sunk fly to obtain good presentation.

rivers are high and the water is cold. This method allows the fly to be offered at the depth where salmon are to be found.

The manner in which the wet fly is presented is dictated basically by the tension on the line and the angle that it is placed upon the water. These factors (in conjunction with the force of the stream flow) control the speed and depth of the offering as it swings across the salmon. There is a certain drill which must be observed when fly fishing for salmon: the line must be cast cleanly, and a good extension of the line, turning over the leader and fly is a necessary requirement for good presentation, giving the angler complete control of the offering from the beginning of the presentational drift of the fly. If the leader does not turn over, but instead drops in loose coils on to the water, the fly is deposited without any line tension to control the drift. It sinks and is carried like a piece of debris with the current and, being out of contact with the pull of the rod, does not hold in the flow and attract the attention of the salmon.

When fishing the wet fly, the line is generally laid on the water, quartering downstream, and is allowed to swing across the flow, while the fly is teased by a rocking movement of the rod. At the end of the drift it is given a moment to hang, is fished back a few feet, picked off, and cast again. There are some who swim the fly without imparting any motion, while others give action to the fly throughout the swinging drift. Both styles take fish, and it must be left up to the angler to experiment and come to his own conclusions. The deeply sunk fly is best fished from a position where the last third of the swing of the cast is occurring in the most likely spot to hold fish, for the fly can be hung over the salmon giving the fish a longer period of observation.

An acutely angled downstream cast will fish the fly much more slowly than a cast executed across the current, which swings the offering at an increasing pace to a point below the angler where it will hang in the flow. The fly, by swinging across the stream, produces a motion which catches the attention of the salmon and, by the mending of the line, the angler can control the pace of the swing executed by the fly on the end of the line. An upstream mend can slow the speed, while a mend made downstream will increase the rate of the swing. In some situations of current flow, mending the line can either help the fly to sink, or lift it to the surface.

The normal procedure when salmon fly fishing is for the angler to use a constant length of line, starting to fish above the chosen spot and to execute three casts — the first at the selected angle, the next with an upstream mend, and the last with a downstream mend (so that the fly is offered at three different speeds and varying depths), after which a short pace downstream is taken and the drill repeated, so that the holding water of the pool is thoroughly covered with the fly.

The sunk fly in high water, on the salmon pool we are using as an example, would be fished from a point opposite the tree stump with the line cast at the angles shown. Attention would be given to the area below the rock, with the fly teased in the pocket of water and the edges of the current. The main holding area of the pool would be the secondary flow of the stream and the fly would be fished in the manner described earlier.

Having established the casting drill and the methods of presenting the fly, there is a final aspect of tackle-handling that should be detailed. A salmon must be allowed time to either turn with the fly after the strike, or take it down from the rise. Many fish are lost by fishermen pulling the line taut too quickly when the acceptance of the fly is detected. My own method is to hold three feet of reserve line which is given to the salmon when it takes the fly before raising the rod to make contact. The style has served me well and I recommend it as a good salmon-fishing practice. I have found this procedure results in the hook taking hold in the scissor part of the mandible, perhaps from the slight downstream bag of line which must occur, but more likely from the fish turning downstream and, as the line draws taut, the fly is pulled to the back of the jaw. The hooks of the salmon fly should be checked during the course of the day and kept needle sharp by rubbing with a hook hone, as a blunt hook is more likely to bounce off a bony part of the jaw than to penetrate it.

Fishing the Wet Fly with a Floating Line

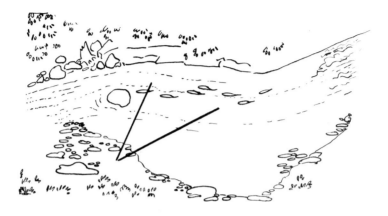

For the shallow-fished wet fly the heavy lines show the angle of drift necessary to cover the fish. Note that the salmon have moved farther across the pool due to the lower water.

The Floating-Line Technique

The next method to be discussed is the style of presentation in which the angler fishes the fly close to the surface. The technique was originated by A. H. E. Wood in the early 1900's and named "greased line," because the silk line was greased so that the fly could be fished high in the water. When water temperatures rise the salmon accept the fly above them more readily than when it is offered at lower depths. Present day technique is still based upon this theory. However, the modern floating and sinking-tip lines have pushed the original name into a nostalgic background, although the style of presentation — a swinging drift without any sudden change of the pace of the fly caused by drag — is occasionally used. Wood's method requires that constant attention be given to the line, with mends thrown during the course of the drift to ensure a drag-free presentation, holding the fly sideways to the current with the rod leading the line — his mends, and controlled drift, achieved by the use of a double-tapered line and a long, two-handed rod.

Reference to the pool diagram, for the floating-line presentation of the wet fly in low water will show that the fish are in new positions and the angle of the cast is less severe, allowing the angler greater versatility in presentational speed and fly action by rod angle, upright or low; leading the line, or following it; and line control (loose snaking casts, line feed, and mending) ; with the fly teased or fished without rod motion.

Today there are two basic methods of a sunk fly presentation — either deeply sunk with the modern high-density line cast at an acute angle, or fished higher in the water with a floating or sinking-tip line cast across the current at a less sharp angle.

There is perhaps one point left that should be emphasized: "drag" when a floating offering is used (dry fly) is the situation when the current pulls the line and draws the fly skidding across the surface; drag, when applied to a salmon wet fly, is actually the stream fishing the offering for the angler by swinging the line which is held by the rod tip downstream across the fish. When salmon fishing with the fly in the upper layers of water, *excessive* drag pulls the fly to the surface and causes it to "skate," a disturbance rather like that a miniature water-skier would make. This should be avoided ("skate" in salmon wet-fly parlance is not the same as the bouncing journey of the dry fly). The manner in which the fly is offered is controlled by the angle at which the line is cast, the amount of loose line used, and the position in which it is placed upon the flow.

Other Styles of Wet-Fly Fishing for Salmon

There are two North American methods of fishing the wet fly that deserve mention. The first is the "Patent" method, which originated on the Restigouche in New Brunswick. For this style of fishing, a large hair-winged Size 3/0 fly is cast upstream on a loose line and allowed to sink and the hair, not being under any pressure from the current, splays out. The fly drifts past the angler and lifts as the line draws tight, a motion which closes the hair. A take can be expected at any stage of the drift and as the style is a favorite method for low-water conditions, it completely upsets the low water/small fly rule.

The second method is the "Hitch," the mechanics of which require, after the leader is tied to the eye, a half-hitch to be looped over the head of the fly, leaving the leader to the side of the river from which it is fished. The swimming action of the fly is heading into the flow, rather than across the current and, when teased, produces a movement that creates attention. It is a method that produces many fish in Newfoundland where the style was evolved. Strangely enough, the method originated in the days of untrustworthy gut-loop-eyed salmon flies. After the leader was tied to the offering, the angler looped a half hitch to the head for additional strength.

If reference is made to the pool diagram, and the angles of line placement for these two methods of presentation studied, it will help emphasize to the angler the importance of the understanding of the presentation of the fly in order to obtain an acceptance.

Dry-Fly Fishing for Salmon

Dry-fly angling for Atlantic salmon is essentially a North American approach to salmon fly fishing and, although the method has been proved to take Icelandic salmon, the style has not been very successful in Britain or Norway. The North American fish, however, will rise to the floated offering quite willingly and the size of the fly used for the method ranges from as small as Size 16 to 1/0, with Size 10 to Size 4 being more generally used.

A dry fly should sit upon the surface rather than lie in the surface film, and the materials employed to dress the large hooks are selected for buoyancy: stiff hackles, resilient hair that repels liquid, and other components chosen for their ability not to absorb water (deer hair, being hollow, is a popular wing and body material).

Flies differ considerably in shape; the Wulff and Irresistible style, the Whiskers and Bomber type, and the Bivisible and Palmer-hackled Bottlewasher variety, all take fish but bear little resemblance to each other, which once more stresses the presentational aspect rather than the imitational approach. (The reader should note that the dry Bomber is a different fly than the wet version of the same name.)

In Europe a fly was developed to simulate a small prawn upon which salmon are known to feed in salt water. It was basically red in tone with a tapered body and head feelers that looked vaguely related to the prawn used by bait-spinning anglers. The fly did take fish, although I feel it received more publicity because of its appearance than its history of success justified. However, the point I wish to make is that a natural prawn has grey transluscence and is saltless, whereas a boiled prawn is red and brined — and this was what the fly imitated! Which I think proves how unpredictable the fancy of a salmon can be and reduces all rules to being simply guidelines from which to start.

The dry fly for salmon is best fished by executing an angled cast made upstream and allowed to drift to a point opposite or slightly below the fisherman, when it is picked off the water with an aerialized roll cast, snapped into a false cast sequence to dry the fly, and placed on to the water again. A lift-off in the normal manner will, more often than not, pull the offering below the surface and waterlog the fly completely. Upstream presentation and downstream drifts can also be used. A "stimulating" method of placing the fly over a known lie, allowing the fly to drift a short distance, picking the fly off, putting it down in the same manner, and repeating the short drift several times, can provoke a salmon to take the fly when it is left to float the full drift.

Now to return briefly to the construction of three dry-fly types. Each provides a different silhouette upon the surface, above the salmon; the dressing styles also supply individual floating characteristics. The Irresistible, for example, can be fluttered, the Bivisible skipped, and the Bomber, because

Three Styles of Canadian Salmon Dry Fly

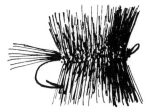

Bivisible

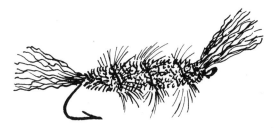

Whiskers

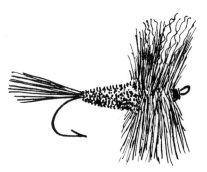

Irresistible

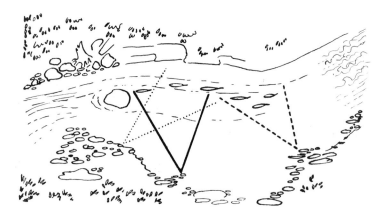

Heavy lines show the presentational drift for the dry fly. Broken lines depict the angle of the cast to fish the Patent method. Dotted lines detail the casting angle for a "hitched" fly.

---

of its shape, wriggled. These are presentational features that should be remembered.

THE ROD

The single-handed fly rod normally fitted with a detachable fighting butt dominates the North American salmon-fishing scene fifty to one, although in Europe the two-handed fly rod is still the favored tool. At an earlier stage in the book, the virtues of both types of rods, together with the mechanics of using them, were discussed and it was established that the longer, twin-handed rod provided more control over the fly, mended the line with greater efficiency, and could be cast from either side of the body (by holding the hand from the side the delivery was to be made uppermost) more easily.

The ability to cast efficiently to the left and the right becomes essential when fishing from the large freighter canoes that are used in North America. The canoe is taken stern-first through a pool in a series of drops, controlled by a bowman with a rope and anchor under the direction of the guide who is seated in the stern. The angler stands or sits in the center of the craft. The fishing drill is to cast alternately to the left and right, starting with only a rod length of line and, after each sequence of casts one to the left, one to the right, extend the line a foot or so, thoroughly covering the water at each side and below the canoe until the maximum amount of line the angler is capable of casting has been reached, after which the canoe is again dropped and the fishing drill repeated.

A long two-handed rod is by far the best equipment to use for this type of North American salmon fishing, as it enables the line to be cast to either side with greater ease and efficiency than can be achieved with the single-handed rod. The additional length of the two-handed rod allows the line to be lifted around and over the stern of the canoe.

FIGHTING AND LANDING THE FISH

For the benefit of anglers who have not experienced hooking and playing a salmon, a brief outline of what may be expected will add greatly to their education. The fly will be swinging on its arc below the fisherman and a strong pull will be felt on the line through the rod, accompanied perhaps by a visible swirl or boil on the water at the spot where the fly is drifting. Three feet of loose line is immediately released and the rod is lifted or swept to the side and, should the salmon have taken the fly, the full weight of the fish will be placed on the rod and the hook will find a hold.

There will be an immediate fast run upstream, terminated by a leap which is the signal to drop the rod and release the tension of the line. A salmon will actually signal a leap, detected through the rod by a slight quiver as the fish gives an extra thrust of speed to lift it from the water. Provided the river is a fair size, the backing line will be through the guides of the arched rod, and the angler may recall during the first electrifying run hearing the click of the backing splice to the main line as it flashed through the rod guides with the reassuring chatter of the reel check in his ears. Line is regained by pumping the rod and drawing the fish towards the angler. A steady pull, lower the rod, wind in the line; lift and pull with the rod, lower and wind in. This will continue until the fish sees the source of the problem in its jaws, and another run and jump can be anticipated. Exactly the same performance will occur when there is an attempt to land the fish: a run not quite so far or so fast — and a tired jump. It is unusual to get a fish to the bank before the second or third attempt. The angler should attempt to play the fish from below, so that the salmon fights both the current and the pull of the rod.

A net or a tailer (a wire snare attached to a three-foot handle) are normally employed to land salmon, although some anglers tail their fish by hand while others beach the fish in a shallow bay with a shingle beach by walking slowly back from the water, getting the fish to swim in the direction of the pull and, even though it may seem strange, the fish will actually swim out of the water up the bank. When fishing from a boat, the craft should be taken to the bank to land the fish, and the salmon brought over the net (rather than the net stabbed at the fish). Or, the salmon should be held steady by the rod, and the looped wire of the tailer moved over the tail and then lifted briskly to set the snare at the junction of body and tail.

CHAPTER 19

The Final Analysis

All over the world, the method of angling with a fly rod is rapidly gaining momentum. The technique is classified by many as being the culmination of the natural angling progression of a fisherman.

The spotted fish caught with a feathered lure cast upon the water first spoken of by Aelian almost two-thousand years ago may have been members of the trout family. It was most certainly the salmonidae group of fishes that encouraged the development of the modern angling form. During the late 1800's, European Brown Trout were introduced to North America, Africa, South America, and New Zealand, while the Rainbow Trout, a native of the West Coast of North America, has enjoyed even greater world-wide distribution. It provides excellent sport for the fly rod as it takes a feathered offering most eagerly: it is a hardy, fast-growing fish and adapts easily to a new geographical location, and the international implantation successes of the Rainbow must place it high on the list of fly-rod sportfish. Rainbow Trout have strong migratory tendencies. The anadromous species found on the West Coast of North America are known as steelhead, and are renowned for the tremendous battle they give the fly fisherman.

As the method of fly fishing became more popular, a greater number of anglers were indoctrinated and, with the realization that all predatory fishes could be taken with a fly, there was a rapid expansion of fly-fishing activity, with all types of piscine predators being pursued by the fly fisherman: bass, tarpon, pike, snook, perch, mackerel, walleye. The only adaption necessary to make the equipment suitable was the addition of a wire or stout nylon section next to the feathered lure when sharp-toothed fish were the quarry.

The techniques which have been discussed can be adapted to all forms of fly fishing, and all types of fish: the slow retrieve of a suitable offering, sunk deeply in still water, will produce walleye, trout, or pike; the long casting, double-haul method is used for big river steelhead fishing; saltwater fly casting and still-water angling enable the fisherman to cover the maximum amount of water; the manipulated dry fly is a style used for trout, perch, and bass; the fast recovery employed with the streamer will take tarpon, bass, char, seatrout, or mackerel . . . it is simply a question of applying one of the basic angling forms to a particular situation. The mechanics of the cast and the function of the equipment remain constant, regardless of the piscine quarry stalked with the feathered offering. Consultation with the charts detailing rod power and tackle application, and a perusal of the fishing technique, will provide the guidance required to explore the angling method with confidence.

The object of this book has been to provide a starting point for those wishing to discover the basics of the angling form, and give the reader some concrete information from which to begin. Fly fishing, with its many facets, is a pursuit that provides the participant with an enormous area of interest, giving the angler a wonderful opportunity of reflection, preparation, and anticipation, and supplying a most gratifying experience to savor in retrospect. It is claimed that angling is a source of mental and physical relaxation, and I would venture to say that fly fishing is even more therapeutic than the other methods. The tackle, casting style, and fishing technique provide the angler with an absorbing pastime.

Perhaps some of the areas reviewed lack the depth of coverage and detail they warrant, however the aim is to provide only the rudimentary knowledge that is required to introduce the angler to the sport. The names of flies, hook sizes, and specific fish types and locations have been purposely ignored to avoid confusion or make the angling method sound complex — it is not. The techniques which have been outlined are a sufficient basis to proceed with the angling form, be it for lake, river, or a saltwater approach. The angler, by simply inquiring as to what type of fly is used and what presentational style is employed to fish it, can start with confidence, for there lies ahead a lifetime of angling pleasure.

Tight Lines!

PHOTO CREDITS

Thanks are due to the following persons and organizations for the use of photographs: Stanley E. Bogdan page 35; Elliott G. Deighton pages 43, 62, 63, 66, 67, 68, 69, 72, 73, 78, 79, 88, 104, 105, 107, 118; Farlow Sharpe pages 19, 25, 29; House of Hardy pages 26, 27, 36, 144, front cover; Tycoon Fin-Nor Corporation page 39; Arthur L. Walker and Son Inc. page 38.

Two Other Important Books from Pagurian Press

JEROME KNAP

THE COMPLETE OUTDOORSMAN'S HANDBOOK

A Guide to Outdoor Living and Wilderness Survival

Everything you need to know for outdoor survival: interpreting animal actions, recognizing poisonous plants and wildlife hazards, understanding a compass and map reading, as well as the skills of canoeing, archery, and snowshoeing.

Jerome Knap is one of the country's foremost outdoor writers. He is also the author of *The Hunter's Handbook, Training the Versatile Gun Dog,* and *Getting Hooked on Fishing.*

JEROME KNAP

WHERE TO FISH AND HUNT IN NORTH AMERICA

Including Mexico and the Caribbean

The Complete Sportsman's Guide

This complete guide is devoted to providing the latest, and most up-to-date information on fishing, hunting, and where to go for best results. Wherever you are or want to go across the United States and Canada, first check out your itinerary with this invaluable guide: what licences are needed, when is open season, what local laws or restrictions must you know, who is a reliable guide, how much will it all cost?